PRAISE

'In *Build, Excite, Equip*, Nicola makes learning how to lead change as fun and welcoming as a chat with a good friend over lunch. In the role of guide, Nicola will help you see potential perils and share her decades of experience so you can both anticipate and navigate the path with ease. Now more than ever, businesses need to build change agility and this book lays an accessible path towards this foundational capability.'

— **Amy Haworth, Corporate Change Practitioner, Global Speaker on Change Management, and former Chief of Staff, HR**

'Nicola Graham is experienced in helping organisations facilitate a shift in behaviour through change management, and it shows. Simple steps and practical tools will help you achieve the same results for your team.'

— **Elizabeth Harrin FAPM, author of *Managing Multiple Projects***

'Nicola has written a great primer for anyone considering business change. *Build, Excite, Equip* is full of important and helpful tools to address the key drivers for ensuring a successful change project.'

— **Alex Christofis, Director of Shared Services and Finance Transformation, The British Land Company PLC**

'When it comes to change and transformation, it is no longer enough simply to have a plan which you execute. We need to think about how we will BEE: how we show up, communicate and connect with stakeholders and the community we are seeking to support through the change. Nicola's *Build, Excite, Equip* will guide you through the process, the plan and the human element of change. There are practical tools and ideas that you can implement immediately, and she generously also gives you access to online tools and processes.'

— **Kirsty Lewis, Founder, School of Facilitation**

HOW TO SIMPLIFY CHANGE
ADOPTION IN YOUR PROJECTS

Build, Excite, Equip.

Nicola Graham

R^ethink

First published in Great Britain in 2022 by
Rethink Press (www.rethinkpress.com)

Dedicated to two of the finest, smartest, most interesting and loving humans walking this planet:

Rhys and Dylan

Thank you for teaching me how to adapt to change every single day.

CONTENTS

Part II Build   29

Part III Excite 99

INTRODUCTION

Welcome Change Leaders. Are your projects meeting their full return on investment? Are your new processes or projects enthusiastically adopted by your colleagues? Do you fancy learning some simple-to-follow steps to help your colleagues adopt the new change quickly and effectively? After all, a happy business is a healthy business.

I wrote *Build, Excite, Equip with* one aim – to change the world of change. My vision for this book was clear: to focus on deliverables and on how to support the project team and the people they're helping, to work together with appreciation for each other. The BEE Methodology© was developed by change managers for project managers, so that those project managers, already masters of technical products and processes, can also become masters of complex transitions and the messy 'people stuff' of business.

Managers create suspicion and detachment towards change processes by holding their cards close to their chest, hushing talk in the break room and canteen, and then simply imposing change on people, handing out thick volumes of instructions written in arcane and inaccessible language, like a 1768 edition of the *Encyclopaedia Britannica*, and expecting everyone to follow. I have found that adapting to change becomes a far more approachable and achievable process when people can talk about what's going on openly and transparently. Change happens all day, every day. It's one of the natural currents of life, but it's whether you go with the flow or fight against the stream that matters.

I'm Nicola Graham, an expert in business change management, transformation and user adoption. I initially focused as a project manager, switching over to the dark side of business change several years ago. During my career I've worked for a wide variety of national and international companies, FTSE 100 companies, large consultancy firms and government organisations including the beautiful British National Health Service (NHS).

I have watched with delight as colleagues of all ages and experiences have embraced the coolest new technologies, adapted to improved processes and organisational restructures and demonstrated their true resilience to company mergers. I've been heavily involved with IT system implementations, from mobile phone apps and bespoke solutions designed in-house, through to big business-critical systems.

My career has meant that, all too often, I have been parachuted into change projects that are failing simply because people haven't been taken along on the journey. I have witnessed incredibly hard-working project teams create wonderful tools and systems that are not then appreciated or utilised by the business. It leaves the potential users frustrated at their lack of involvement and the poor communication, leading to resistance towards the project team and their ideas. Seeing this problem from both sides has left me wondering, how can I mitigate this?

Build, Excite, Equip is my solution. I have written this book as an introduction to my easy-to-follow BEE Methodology, an acronym for Build, Excite, Equip. Each of these phases consists of three uncomplicated stages: Organisation/People/Project; Create/Inform/Market; Develop/ Educate/Invigorate. Working your way through these ensures you stay on track as you progress through your change journey. If you're looking for undecipherable jargon and complicated graphs, I apologise in advance because I can't help you: BEE is a straightforward methodology that makes business change collaborative and non invasive. I hope you enjoy simplicity as much as I do.

My aim is to simplify change management activities to enable project teams to deliver the type of outcomes that would normally require a business change manager. This book aims to bridge the gap between the project people and the businesspeople. This mitigates the risk of the change project frustrating the people (and the people potentially frustrating the project in return) and will hopefully bring the project teams some well-deserved kudos along the way.

I cover the basics of business change management in this book, considered simply and without the complication of unnecessary jargon. Through this, I will show you new perspectives on your role as a change initiator and leader so that you can take on the position of a business change manager. Whether you're part of a project team, head of a department or even someone looking to move into a more transformational role, this book is for you. If you are working on a project – be that a system or process change – that will require people to accept and/or use this change, you need to take them on the journey with you. What that means in simple terms is that you need to involve people from the start of your project and take the time to understand the impact your project will have on them. The BEE Methodology ensures this is done via a step-by-step process to:

- **Build** a plan to alleviate fear and set the engagement plan in motion

- **Excite** the people with good communication so they buy into the change

- **Equip** them with the tools they need to learn about the change

The BEE way of business change entails the following:

- Sticking close to the reality of your work life, which means keeping it real and relatable with straightforward language and explanations

- Giving you practical and straightforward guidance on how to approach business change with the people in your organisation

- Providing clear explanations of what to do, how to do it, when to do it and why

The BEE Methodology can be used on a project of any size and type, be that a digitalisation change, a new IT system, a company restructure or a process change. I present every part of BEE in this book, of course, but feel free to use only individual components of the methodology if that's all your specific project needs to ensure a project change happening to the people is accepted and adopted by the people.

Build, Excite, Equip.

I really hope you enjoy this book, and that it helps give you enhanced social currency within your organisation. Remember, I love to learn about people, know their stories and hear their experiences, so I invite you to reach out to me and share yours.

PART I
GETTING STARTED

1

THE BASICS OF CHANGE

ROLES AND REASONS

Let's take a look at the key roles in a change project, including the most important players of all, the people who are affected by the change.

A business change manager's role

I am often asked what exactly is a 'business change manager' so here's my elevator pitch:

> Have you ever been in a situation where you have arrived at work one day and the core system that you've used for years has suddenly changed? It makes you feel flustered, disrupted, confused and frustrated, right? Well, in my role as a business change manager, I stop this from happening by working within the project team to understand what impact this change will have on your role and that of your colleagues, putting steps in place to ensure you all receive the support you need to be ready for that change.

In a slower explanation, what this means is that a business change manager focuses on understanding what the impact will be, on an individual level, of moving from the 'current state' to the 'future state', ie what are the people doing now and what will be the impact of the change for them, their position and their responsibilities? This is a role that often requires lots of support from a business change project team, which includes communication leads, change analysts, trainers and project support. A good business change manager will ask 'Why?': Why are we changing, what are the benefits to the people and why should they embrace this change? Each person has different needs and abilities, but a change project may impact hundreds, maybe even thousands, of people, so categorising people into different persona types (often known as 'change players') helps to focus on supporting each type of individual's needs.

A business change manager will work with senior management teams to rally supporters for the change who will help influence and encourage their colleagues who are going through the change. They will also work with the project team to provide the people's voice, so that the users' requirements are addressed during the project; *fancy having a process or system that does exactly what you need it to do – nice thought, huh?* The business change manager will then create strong supportive engagement plans to spread the news about the change that is happening and ensure that the training is provided and learning needs are met for everyone. Most importantly, I put the champions and influencers (or 'change agents' as I refer to them in the book) in place to embed change to ensure it sticks. This is the 'checkmate' of all good change plans.

I often describe the attributes required of a business change manager as being like a box of chocolates with a variety of different flavours (or skills). The role is a composite of co-ordinator, salesperson, spokesperson, marketeer, translator, empath, psychologist, coach, motivator and mediator – all bundled up in one role, ready to work within a team to help people embrace change.

A change manager is also a governing role within a project. If a project manager requests a change to their project plan (time, quality or cost of the project) then a change manager evaluates the impact of this change, leading to an approval or rejection of that change. It is true that a change manager will often engage with a business change manager (a little cross-eyed statement there, I'll give you a moment with that...) to understand the impact that this project change will have on the business and implementation plans.

Project team's roles

Throughout this book we will be discussing the following roles within a project team:

- **Business change manager:** responsible for the strategic planning and implementation of all change activities.

- **Project manager:** responsible for the three key areas of time, quality and cost; manages the controls within the project to ensure it runs smoothly. *Spoiler alert: my aim in this book is for the people adoption to become part of this.*

- **Change analyst:** think business analyst but focused on the change activities required for gathering data and information about the change management plan. It is my recommendation that you use existing business analysts within your project to take on this role as it tends to need the attention to detail and ability to extract information that these guys possess.

- **Change agents:** the 'James Bonds' of your change activities. I use 'change agents' as the collective term for the businesspeople that we discuss in two main roles:

  - **Change influencers:** a person in the business recognised as an advocate for the change, someone with a strong presence so that they can communicate the change to the business.

  - **Change champions:** a person within the business who is enthusiastic, quick to learn and eager to encourage others to support and adapt to the change.

- **Communication lead:** someone superb at writing, ready to assist you with communicating your engagements. You may already have someone in this role, or you may need to lean on an articulate person within the project to help implement the advice we give throughout this book.

- **Training lead:** trainers are specialists in themselves. I wouldn't advocate taking on this role lightly, but you can follow the guidance in this book to apply some 'smart' training ideas. Lean on your Learning and Development (L&D) or Human Resources (HR) teams to help here, if need be.

- **Organisation/business/people/colleagues/key stakeholders:** these are all terms referencing the individuals accepting and impacted by the change happening in your project.

People return on investment

Now let's look at why taking people along on the project journey is so important. Why should a project manager worry what the people think, or want to understand the impact that this project will have on them? After all, surely the key considerations for a project are to focus on delivering on time, at the budgeted cost and to the expected standard of quality, aren't they? Here is a little fact for you, 70% of projects that are directly used by people fail to meet their return on investment if the people are not engaged along the way.[1] What this suggests is that there is, in fact, a 'people return on investment' that is directly linked to the project's return on investment.

A business change plan should always be written with success criteria, so ask yourself, how often do your project success criteria relate to uptake, increase or usage? In my project management experience of many a project closure meeting these successes aren't always met efficiently, and this is too often due to lack of people engagement.

Still not totally convinced? Think of it this way: imagine a project that is building and selling houses. The return on investment to the property developer is to have people buy the houses, correct? As a property developer, I invest £2 million, and expect to start selling houses on 1 January, which is my go-live date. Let's look at some simple steps I can take to ensure my return on investment is successful:

- Understand your area, engage with local people and identify their needs to ensure that you are providing the correct type of property. For example, if there are lots of families, you'll need to build houses or community builds; if the area is populated by working professionals, flats would be more appealing. Learn how to create, design and market the benefits of your development to this target audience.

- Start advertising early by putting up billboards at the building site and arranging adverts in local papers, online search engines and property websites.

- Create a show home or centre to showcase the quality and finish to enhance people's desire to buy the homes.

- Equip the buyers with all the information they need to be able to mortgage the properties, facilitating their decision to purchase one.

With this strategy in place, people buy the properties off the plan, the properties are ready on 1 January, and the return on investment is being met right from the launch date.

Now imagine this same example, but without any of the steps above. The properties are ready on 1 January as the project team did a great job at producing quality homes on time and on budget. However, the buyers are not engaged, so 1 January arrives and you realise that you haven't sold your homes. It's only then that you start taking steps to promote and advertise your homes, so your return on investment is delayed for months until you finally sell the homes, rather than seeing instant returns on the go-live date.

In any project that creates something that is to be directly used by the people, those people will have an impact on the project's success and the return on investment achieved. You can be managing a project that is creating the best solution for people, saving them time and effort, reducing risks, creating well-being and so on, but if they don't know it exists, the benefits they'll receive or how to use it, your project solution is essentially worthless.

Let's take people on your project's journey together and improve your project's chance of success and return on investment.

Individual responses to change

Change is a constant in life. We're all changing every single day, but the irony of change is that the moment it is forced upon us, it highlights our lack of choice or agency, and this begins to have an impact on us. I'll look closely at the neuroscience of change later, but I feel that it is important at this stage to emphasise that how we respond to change will vary on an individual basis, and culture, age, personal circumstances and intellectual curiosity will all play a part in each person's journey.

While this book is about how business in general can adapt and adopt change, our current era of digital disruption provides a great example of how change is impacting the IT sector. Digital innovations such as big data, machine learning, the switch to cloud technologies and so on are causing huge transformations on an individual, organisational, industry and societal levels.

Let's take a moment here to think about the organisational disruption it causes us. The working world consists of over five decades of people working together, all adapting to this rapid pace of technology disruption. The impact is huge, and often forced upon us, which can create resistance to change. Take a moment to consider the changes your colleagues are going through right now in your organisation. How many initiatives, launches and changes are they being put through on a regular basis? How do you think it makes them feel? How do you think it makes them feel towards the projects being forced upon them, and why? If we can all align a little more by thinking about the 'Why', we may begin to bridge the gap between project teams and frustrated users. This is why I created the BEE Methodology. In any case, expect to be a little transformed yourself.

Summary

Business change, regardless of scale, always involves several key players. However, critical to my BEE approach is an understanding that people must be the focus of every one of these positions. Whichever hat you wear, make sure you understand your role in helping people adapt to change.

2

SETTING EXPECTATIONS

A MANAGEMENT OUTLOOK

There is far more 'people' stuff to project management than simply putting together a project team and directing their efforts. There's a human dimension to projects aimed at business change, and those affected could experience a real rollercoaster of emotions, including fear, doubt, resistance, curiosity, acceptance and even euphoria. The people who are, willingly or not, being taken along for the change ride need genuine attention and sensitive handling, because how people respond to the challenges your change project poses to their professional lives will ultimately determine your success in creating a lasting impact with your work.

In this chapter, I'll look at the importance of understanding how people work together, and of gaining their trust for the change journey ahead.

Stretching into new skills

When leading a change project, alongside your official title as business change manager, you will probably also find yourself wearing many other hats. You'll find yourself taking on multiple roles at the same time (haven't you always wanted to be both a hero firefighter and a mysterious fortune teller?) and probably find yourself initiating and co-ordinating activities that go well beyond what you can currently envisage – and your current job description, for that matter. It's therefore immediately obvious that this is an opportunity for personal development and upskilling to give your career that extra bit of spice.

Say this to yourself (out loud if possible) because that'll help you believe it: this is an opportunity to grow

Now, take a moment to imagine yourself:

- Tracing back social network maps and analysing stakeholder engagement in your company, like an anthropologist studying an ancient society

- Dissecting and examining the individual components of your project like a biologist trying to understand an organism under a microscope

- Mapping out the project timeline and milestones, like a travel agent designing a summer holiday's itinerary and activities

- Knocking on every door like a potential election candidate to proselytise about the greatness of the change that is about to happen

- Promoting the heck out of the new solution's advantages and benefits like the marketing manager of a football club trying to fill the home stadium

- Creating a roar in the hallways like the event manager of a new festival that the world has been waiting for (please don't take the FYRE Festival as your inspiration for this one).

- Giving people the opportunity to cultivate their digital skills and learn to navigate a whole new world like Dumbledore's mentorship of Harry Potter

- Building and maintaining new communication channels across the entire company, like the invention of the walkie-talkie or even the telephone about a million years ago

As a business change manager, you can do all those things. Not only do you have your entire project team at your side, present and ready to kill it, but you've also got an organisation full of talented individuals who have expertise in just the things you're looking for. All the resources you need are already there. You just need to know who to ask.

What is certainly beyond doubt is that this transformation is bigger than just a process upgrade, and that, from this day forward, you will be so much more than 'just' a project manager.

The power of collaboration: When two and two equals five

As you get started on this journey, don't look too closely at your job description. As this change project unfolds, you will find that having a business change agenda suddenly gives you a whole new place in your organisation. You will also realise that there's a whole cavalry of talented people out there with just the expertise you need, even if you're not yet aware of what you need or who they are. This is going to be important to remember later in this journey.

For those who do serious research on the topic (and whose slightly intimidating academic language I won't adopt here, don't worry), collaboration is considered to be the process of working together, in the process generating a synergy that brings significant advantage. Collaboration means joining efforts to achieve outcomes greater than those that can be achieved by individuals alone. It means creating something that is bigger than the sum of its parts, and cultivating a sense of belonging within the collaborating teams and across whole organisations.[2,3,4] Sounds exactly like what you'd need: to create something big, make the changes so that you don't have to pull all that weight alone.

Here is our first lesson: lasting change is a collaborative effort.

Change as a collaborative mission

Collaboration, by definition, cannot be done alone. You could work with Alex from Public Relations (PR) to create a watertight business change communication strategy, ask Kim from Marketing to help with event co-ordination, request a quick lesson over lunch on the art of developing talent from Neela in HR, and consult with Ahmad from Customer Service for tips on handling complaints; include anyone who has valuable expertise on anything that could make your life as a project manager, and the lives of those affected by the change, significantly easier. Don't overcomplicate it though.

A 2012 study by the innovative design company HermanMiller – who really know their stuff when it comes to interaction in the workplace – found that there's a good amount of variation in how collaboration happens.[5] It is often spontaneous, a little chaotic, unplanned and undefined. *Refreshing, no?* The study shows that collaborative encounters are mostly between two or three people, 34% of cases last less than fifteen minutes (less than thirty minutes in 60% of cases), and don't require any fancy tools. As the study notes, 'when people want to collaborate, they seek out the simplest, most convenient solution'[6] – such effectiveness.

What's important is that you remember this throughout the entire course of the project: achieving lasting business change is not something that you, or you and your project team, have to do alone. Working together across the whole organisation, pulling in those with niche expertise and openly asking for each other's support is key to moving forward with any business change agenda. You want to be doing this with people, not for people.

You have even got neurobiology on your side. It so happens that helping others releases feel-good neurotransmitters like oxytocin, which are basically pleasure chemicals, in the reward reinforcement systems of our brains, giving us a distinct sensation of happiness and inducing a so-called 'helper's high', which can even lead to 'greater health and increased longevity'.[7]

Changing things up: A matter of trust

One more thing before I dive into the practicalities of business change. Rattling the cage – as you are about to do with your business change agenda – may not just loosen things a little; beware that it has the potential to completely disrupt people's working realities.

Trust is a complex subject, explored by biologists, anthropologists, psychologists and a whole host of other people that we're not going to mention now. To keep it simple, I'll explore trust just from an economic perspective (although we know this is just one of many). Harvard Business School professor Frances Frei describes trust between humans as a delicate interplay of authenticity, logic and empathy.[8] She argues that you are far more likely to trust someone if they seem authentic, if you sense that their logic is truly rigorous, and if you believe that they are empathetic towards you.

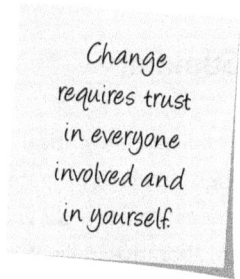

Change requires trust in everyone involved and in yourself

Now, trust between two individuals is one thing, but having trust in a whole organisation is another altogether. Trust is a vast human concept, endlessly complex and impossible to make tangible, visible or quantify. PricewaterhouseCoopers reported that 55% of chief executive officers (CEO) consider a lack of trust within an organisation a serious threat to its growth.[9]

One little thing that you can do in the context of your business change project is to take to heart the idea of robust logic – something you're probably already extremely good at. Ensure your plans and actions are based on absolutely sound logic, reasoning and rationales and communicate these arguments to every single person in your organisation who is affected by the change. Do this in your own words, but in ways that people understand. Try to be in their shoes for a minute while you're at it.

Here is a quick set of recommendations for how to build more trust into your business change agenda:

- Communicate: clearly and regularly, and more than you think even possible.

- Stick to your word: if change can't be predictable, at least you can be reliable in its delivery.

- Be transparent and honest: here is one magic word: integrity.

- Extend your trust to others: trust is a mutual thing, period.

Summary

People are the critical element of any change project. You need to consider their needs, anticipate their reactions to change and win them over to the cause. How do you do that? By building trust. Remember, change is collaborative; delight in the moment that you realise you are not alone in this journey.

3

BEE

AN OVERVIEW

I've developed the BEE program to guide you through the process of change, bringing people along with you every step of the way, but before we explore it in detail, let's first get an overview of BEE.

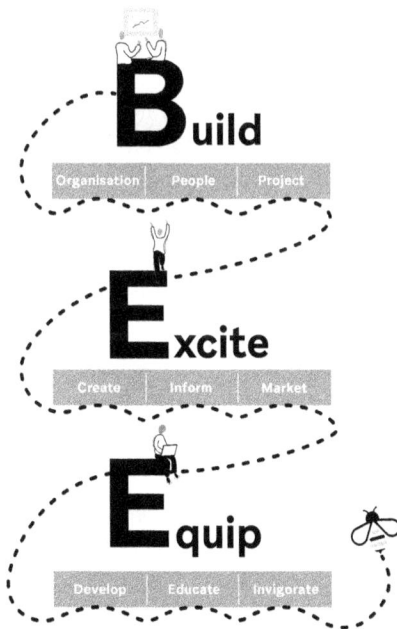

What is BEE?

I know that project managers are already experts in technical products and processes, so I developed the BEE Methodology to help them become equally skilled in managing the messy people stuff and complex transitions. Sometimes people can be as mysterious as the variable x, and transitions don't just happen overnight – even if that would be extremely nice and save you a lot of nerves.

This is a guide, straightforward and unpretentious, for those who have no idea how to approach their business change; it is an inspiration for those who are just beginning to build a business change project, and an encouragement for those who'd like to do more for the people they're confronting with change. It is for those who are exploring opportunities for business change, those who have already started, those who have already gotten stuck, and those who want to prevent themselves from getting stuck again in the future.

Why choose BEE?

While adjustments to technical processes can be carefully mapped out in advance and followed through in a linear fashion, change processes that involve people (aka emotional beings and creatures of habit) are largely unpredictable and highly complex.

We're all different people, doing different jobs with different responsibilities, and working in different ways albeit potentially using the same technical tools, and yet these differences are often completely disregarded in project planning. This is not because it is driven by an evil project manager who would like nothing more than to see the world go up in flames, but because introducing people to

A whole different profession. A whole different perspective. That's exactly where the BEE Methodology comes in.

fundamental change in their working lives is the job of a business change manager.

The BEE Methodology lets you see your projects through a business change manager lens by integrating the complex and unpredictable 'people' side of change with the technical and calculable 'product' or 'process' side. It acknowledges the necessity of hard planning in project management as part of your job, but it also helps you think through the likely responses, emotions and potential actions of the people whose working lives are about to catch fire.

How does BEE work?

I try to keep it simple. Not because I want to ignore the complexity and messiness of business change (obviously), but because I don't believe in unnecessary jargon and complicated graphs that make everyone's heads spin.

The BEE Methodology makes business change management accessible by using everyday language and a combination of explanations, exercises and examples. It helps you facilitate new ways of working, taking the people along with you rather than just imposing change upon them. I use insights from my own experience as a project manager and a business change consultant (plus all the frustration with inflated strategies that I've felt along the way) to guide you through the process of building a foundation for your project, exciting the masses and equipping people to make the change work. *Build - Excite - Equip.*

Remember that.

Integrating BEE with project management plans

Every business change project has its own quirks and twists. Project management structures vary from one company to another: I often find myself playing the 'How many stages does your project office have?' game. Trends, legislation, company policies and immediate responses to current events inevitably make it that way.

Given no two projects are the same, I'm not going to give you absolute answers in this book. To do so would be not only extremely presumptuous of me, but also completely irresponsible because neither you nor I can anticipate how the process of applying change within your specific project is going to unfold. One thing I would like to share with you, however, is the concept of how you can integrate the BEE Methodology into your project governance to ensure that you are achieving milestones and reaching goals along the way.

Here is a rough outline of how the BEE phases, the exercises and project milestones come together in a typical five-stage project framework.

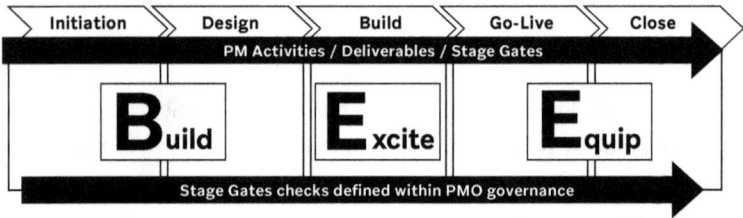

An outline of how the three BEE phases sit within a five-stage project framework

As we go through each section, I will begin to build on this basic framework and add in deliverables and activities that you may wish to include. I will guide you through the methodology, focusing on several different areas and introducing guidelines to help you get your project change ready. Along the way I will use a fictional company, River Construction, as a case study to demonstrate how the methodology has helped real-life clients.

You will find plenty of references throughout the book to free-to-use resources, including videos, assessments, instructions on how to collect and analyse data, and examples of our work; you can access these using the QR codes within the text.

See our case study examples:

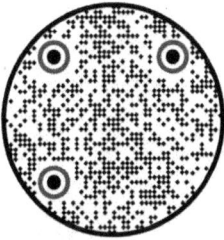

BEE Insights: Business change management software

I know that managing a business change project can sometimes feel like spinning plates. The amount of hard work and brain exercise it takes to get a holistic understanding of what's going on at your organisation and with your people goes far beyond the day-to-day business of a project manager. And that's the point. You're on the way to becoming a business change manager – more of a people's person. You're upskilling into a whole new qualification level.

It's only natural that this can seem like a whole lot to juggle right now. Learning processes like this can be overwhelming and require commitment, energy and nerves of steel. While you're upgrading your project management skills to take on some of the role of a business change manager, I suggest lightening your load a little to make sure you don't burn out before achieving the real rewards for all your hard work. If possible, delegate the technical and practical matters of the process so that you can gain a little capacity for the development of your soft skills – your ability to work with people. I'll help you work on these, including skills such as communicating empathetically and engaging effectively, because I know how truly valuable they will prove to be once we move into BEE's Excite and Equip phases.

One way of making time during the initial Build phase is to appoint someone as your change analyst. They can help with searching for suitable questionnaire tools that allow you to gather the data needed (including transferring questions from our PDFs into such tools), sending out the link and chasing responses, exporting and analysing the data and creating insightful visualisations of the results. I provide detailed instructions on what to do and how, so even an inexperienced intern would be able to see this process through.

I've spent days and nights doing exactly that work, and to be quite honest, most of the time I was simply crossing my fingers and hoping for the best. If it can be its own job with someone thinking about nothing but internal research, then that's great; if it must be managed alongside business as usual, you're in for more juggleries.

> Give it a fancy name: Business Change Data Analysis Intern. Voilà, you've got yourself the perfect position for an eager university student on a semester break.

Data puzzles take a lot of energy. Unfortunately, all too often they create merely a pile of data garbage when what you really need is a bit of data magic to better understand your organisation, your people and your project.

My solution to find this 'data magic' is BEE Insights, a web-based tool especially made for data collection and analysis in the Build phase of the BEE Methodology. BEE Insights is a super-simple tool with a clean user interface and contains all the questionnaires necessary for the complex and crucial surveys you'll need, including the Organisation Assessment, the Key Stakeholder Engagement Evaluation, the Social Network Analysis, Communication Channels, Change Freeze Analysis, Learning and Development and the Adoption Success Rating and so on. All you need to do is distribute the questionnaires within your organisation, sit back and wait for the answers to populate, and then let the software automate the filing and compilation of people's responses, before providing you with instant visualisations of the data. A one-stop-shop tool like this comes in particularly handy if collecting data at scale, and it will guide you on what you might want to do with the data and how it can be implemented in the next phases of the BEE Methodology.

Try the BEE Insights tool here:

Summary

BEE stands for:

1. **Build:** analyse and plan

2. **Excite:** market and communicate

3. **Equip:** train and reinforce

By breaking the process down into these clearly defined steps, I've developed an extremely straightforward approach to guide you through the change process. I align the methodology with a project management framework that you should adapt to suit your organisation. I have developed hands-on resources, questionnaires and tools for different stages in this process which are detailed in the 'Exercises' chapters that occur after the stages within the phases. I've also provided a case study of how to implement the process through the full life cycle of a project in our 'River Construction' examples.

All the way along, I keep it simple, accessible and unpretentious and I'll walk you through every step of the way.

PART II
BUILD

Build

| Organisation | People | Project |

4

THE BUILD PHASE

FOUNDATIONS FOR THE FUTURE

When I think of the Build phase of the BEE Methodology, those early stages of a business change project, I cannot help but think of a classic game of chess. Not so much the apparent simplicity imposed by the clear black-and-white squares or the absolute certainty that one of two people will win, but rather the chess player's game strategies that are developed long before they sit down at the table, the mindset that they descend into when they touch the first piece, and the elegant series of actions and reactions that lead to complex and orchestrated victories.

I think of self-awareness and forward thinking, a game that is played out in the moment while simultaneously planning fifteen to twenty moves ahead. I think of the attention to detail required to build a flexible and adaptable battleplan with a multitude of contingencies before getting ready to attack. I think of the intentionality of it all, how everything builds up to a careful but confident execution in a temporary world of endless possibilities – it's truly inspirational.

What I really mean is that the Build phase establishes this vision of your business change project as a configuration of past, present and future moves. You can't make winning moves if you don't know your territory, and you can't win if you don't know the rules.

What is the Build phase?

The Build phase takes a deep dive into analysing your organisation, your people and your project plans. It is about establishing a detailed and accurate understanding of the status quo at your organisation so that you can then formulate plans to progress and advance. This includes documenting the hard facts of your organisation, assessing the roles within it, coming to understand what motivates your people and deciding how to position your project with a view to the future.

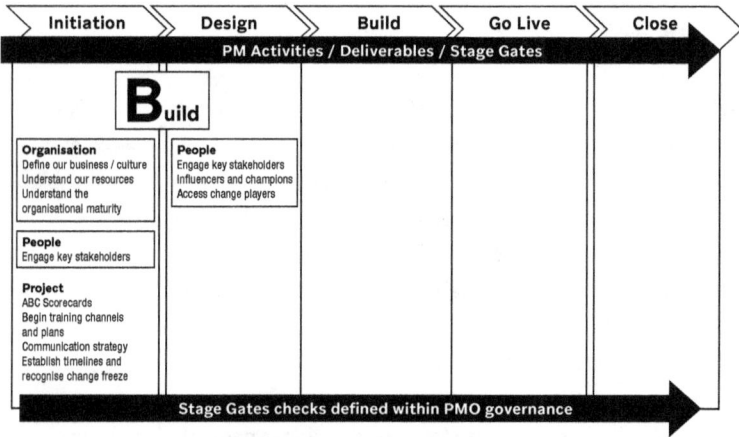

How Build can overlay your project framework

In the Build phase you will consider things under three broad headings:

- **Organisation**

  — Define your business and culture.

  — Understand the resources you currently have available.

  — Understand the maturity of the organisation.

- **People**

  - Define your key stakeholders.

  - Recognise the influencers and champions.

  - Access the change players.

- **Project**

  - Implement the ABC Scorecards.

  - Begin establishing training channels and plans.

  - Create your communication strategy.

  - Establish timelines and recognise change freezes.

A close analysis

To begin the process of establishing how business change can be achieved at your organisation, you need first to understand the position as it is now. This requires scrutiny of everything around you, observation so detailed and deliberate that you find yourself able to see and really understand how things are being done at your organisation (as opposed to how they officially should be done, which is a whole different story). This probably sounds highly abstract and unrealistic right now, maybe even quite intimidating, but I promise that it will become clear as we work through the following exercises and examples together. After all the building work is done, what you'll end up with is a 'people and process database' that will be your reference point for everything that concerns your business change agenda for the life cycle of the project.

But why, you may wonder, should you care about the current situation? Isn't this just extra work, and aren't we all leading incredibly busy working lives already? Good questions.

Reasons to Build

1. Everything that you do before you get the change project ball rolling smooths the path for faster action and easier adoption later. It is as simple as that.

2. Adding layers of cross-departmental collaboration will turn into complete anarchy if you don't have a bird's eye perspective on, and a clear understanding of, the entire mission, start to finish.

3. Understanding the present state of everything at your organisation gives you a massive head start in constructing a logical change narrative for the people. Rigour in logic helps build trust, remember?

4. Turning over every stone between interns and management, Accounts and Marketing, the canteen and the home offices is the perfect context for promoting critical thinking and creative problem solving, qualities that you'll need a lot of from now on. Athletes warm up before the competitions, so should you.

5. Scouting the terrain and understanding where you are currently helps to turn uncertainty into certainty, or at least making that uncertainty less ambiguous and mysterious. That's a tremendous way to ensure you're providing support for people accepting change.

6. There are things about your organisation and the way things work that you don't yet know – surprises come as freebies in business change projects.

Planning

The American business administration scholars Harold Koontz and Cyril O'Donnell were fascinated by the possibilities and potential of long-range planning in business: 'Planning is deciding in advance what to do, why to do, when to do, how to do and who is to do it. Planning bridges the gap between where we are and where we want to go.'[10] Anyone can understand that. It is making an action plan before the action happens. Sounds not only straightforward and doable, but also rational and reasonable.

This definition can, however, be usefully expanded: planning is a cognitive process, a conscious intellectual activity with a future-focus that aids in schematising resources and strategising the achievement of a desired outcome.

There are two types of plans:[11]

1. Those that are an organisation of knowledge and help build an understanding of the current situation – the resource kind

2. Those that serve as a guide to how to get somewhere else, laying out a set of priorities, objectives and specified goals – the strategy kind

During the Build phase, you will be doing a whole lot of the first kind of planning: collecting and analysing data from within the organisation to gain a better understanding and knowledge of the current state of affairs. You'll see that organising knowledge to understand the status quo naturally leads to the second type of plans, guides to action that outline where to go and how to get there, which form the foundation of your business change project. The kind of knowledge I'm talking about here applies to most of the exercises you will do as you get started on the Build phase. The kind of action that needs to happen is then captured as part of the training and communication plans, which are part of routine project management work.

The reason why we're going to go to the trouble of first organising knowledge is that the composition and analysis of specially requested information allows us – you – to understand your organisation's socio-professional fabric, the all-too-important knots on the grapevine (because there is one, believe me...), the official and unofficial communication channels, and the overall attitude towards your project.

You will find the ringleaders and hear the gossip. Brace yourself.

This will guide your understanding of what (or who) should be the focus of your time and energy, what to work towards and what boxes to check along the way. It will provide a new perspective to the kind of project (and action) planning you might be familiar with. It really helps to break this beast of a mission down into manageable elements that encourage discipline and process. Change, but bite-sized.

The Project Management Institute reported that the primary cause of failure (37%) for a strategic initiative is the 'lack of clearly defined objectives and milestones to measure progress'.[12] Consider this a small statistical splinter in the grand scheme of things; a quick reality check to quantify the world of strategic initiatives. The best takeaway point here would be: Have an action plan so good, any SWAT team would be impressed. Or at least make it complete, efficient and fool proof, if uniforms and special effects are out of the question.[13]

Have your current plans handy and take notes as you go through the book, add items, activities and update your timeline.

Summary

The Build phase will lay the foundation for your change project. It will establish a realistic insight into your organisation's status quo, including its formal and informal structures, its social networks and relationships. It will also set out the plans that will guide your project to completion. There are three components:

- **Organisation:** Map the organisation's structures, including both the formal and the informal structures.

- **People:** Analyse people and their social networks and understand how individual reactions to business change work.

- **Project:** Define what you mean by success and determine how you will schedule it, track it and use it to inform your action plans.

I make elaborate plans to understand the resources of the present, to craft a more robust strategy for the future. For any business change journey to be successful, it's critical to be clear on the departure point, as well as the destination, if we are to accurately calculate our direction of travel.

5

ORGANISATION

THE GRAND SCHEME OF THINGS

To begin our Build phase, the first thing you'll need to do is to zoom out to get oversight of the entire picture, even if that means making extra time on an already tight-as-heck schedule and runs counter to your fast-paced mentality. By taking a minute, stepping back and looking at the bigger picture, you're basically shoving a game manual and strategy sheet up your sleeve for later. These guides are going to be invaluable once you've set everything in motion and you need to make quick decisions on what to do with your time and who to ask for a little favour. This is when you put the chessboard on the table and get ready to play.

Wait and see. Plan and become victorious.

The official story

Allow yourself to zoom out, away from the budget plans and software, project teams and departments, divisions and regions, and even however much further you need to go to get away from the context of your organisation and project. Take it all in: this is the wider context in which you're about to initiate business change. Make a mental note to consider how far your project could, should or will reach within the organisation. It's like getting a feel for the strategies that you'll play by (some of which you will have to invent yourself, I'll have you know) and understanding the size of the chessboard: while chessboards are 8x8 squares in the world of mind sports, there are all kinds of different sized boards in the world of change management.

What I do to work through this conundrum is first document the official structures and pathways within your organisation, and then slowly zoom back in to get a better look at the details. Your notes should include everything from the formal hierarchy, company size and locations, to the existence of a communications team and the state of training systems. A bunch of

Your change management board might just be 7x12 squares. What are you going to do about it?

formalities, if you will, that help you gain a fuller understanding of how things should officially work and who *should* be linked together.

I took the liberty of preparing a couple of exercises that might be helpful for your investigation; detailed instructions follow at the end of this section. Use the Corporate Survey to establish the hard facts of the organisation and follow the instructions to create an Organisational Chart that visualises your company's formal setup, with identification of all divisions, departments, teams and people in charge.

The actuality

When you take a bird's eye perspective on the official structure of your organisation, you're looking only at the surface, the company's public face. By establishing this official version, you are getting a glimpse of the general instructions in the chess manual; understanding the hard rules is

May the fun begin with a little desk research. May there be enough coffee to see you through.

essential to playing the game well, whether that be chess or corporate politics. However, zooming back in to take a closer look is how you gain an insight into how things *actually* work and what people are *really* doing; this part of the manual is the strategy and tactics, with room for individual interpretation, ingenuity and freestyle manoeuvres. This 'corporate cleverness' is the unwritten laws and tricks of project management and business change, and this is key to winning the game. See what's happening? There is stuff written between the lines here.

You need to set up an investigation (this time bring your detective hat) to find out as much as possible about the unwritten reality of working within your organisation. The emphasis here is on the working environment that your organisation has cultivated and how people feel about changes in that environment, which will give you an idea of the overall climate for your anticipated business change. Start digging deeper into individual positions within the organisation and analysing what those different perspectives mean for your project. I know that it's hard to know all the details and even harder to formulate appropriate responses, but I'm right here with you, guiding you along the way. You want to do this right.

So, grab the Organisation Assessment (see Chapter 6), send it to as many people as you can in your organisation, and use your irresistible charm to get them to answer the 'aha' questions because you need something to work with. You need to know if your organisation is generally ready for (yet another) business change, if people feel confident using communication and information technology, how people like to receive their information, how big of a disruption your project is to them, and how much people want to learn about new stuff.

Let me just say that now is probably your one and only chance to get a full understanding of this, because later you'll be one busy change manager with not a minute to spare to go back and find out whether Billie and the team in Operations prefer to be kept in the loop via email or messenger.

A reality check

Before you rush off to get this first set of exercises done, I should take a second to remind you of the context that we're about to confuse/disrupt/ enlighten (choose your poison) with business change. We're likely looking at an organisation that has been an established business for many years, with an intricately tested and approved order of operations and many people doing everything in their power to keep everything running smoothly – a normal organisation, the kind that's always been there and is serving its purpose, day in and day out. Maybe the kind in which two out of three change endeavours fail.

The longer an organisation has been operating in its one particular way, the more fossilised the whole thing has become over the years and decades; *'Plus ça change, plus c'est la même chose'* ('The more things change, the more they stay the same'), according to the French writer, Jean-Baptiste Alphonse Karr.[14] There's therefore a really good chance that you're looking at a fixed and inflexible machine that's humming and trotting along like it always has. It is not an environment that seems ready and willing to embrace change, but history and tradition should never be allowed to stand in the way of progress; this is why, in 2016, 'This is the way we've always done it' were declared the nine 'most dangerous words in business'.[15]

Summary

The structure of an organisation includes both an 'official' version (the business structure) and the 'unofficial' side (the unwritten systems and processes at play in the workplace). You can use my Corporate Survey and Organisational Chart to map the former, and the Organisation Assessment to reveal the latter.

6

EXERCISES: ORGANISATION
THE ORGANISATION TOOLS

Mapping the structures in your organisation is easy with our three key tools – the Corporate Survey, the Organisational Chart and the Organisation Assessment.

The Corporate Survey

Let us begin with an easy one, the corporate fact-check, an exercise so easy that it really doesn't need instructions. Some parts of the survey you might be able to answer in your sleep, like describing your organisation's industry or the number of employees (if not, a quick glance at your organisation's website should do the trick). Some sections, however, might require more research or even a little help from the experts. I would always recommend double checking your facts with Neela from HR or Billie from Operations. I'd also recommend sitting down to talk through the survey with a senior manager, for two reasons. First, they're likely to be most familiar with the facts that you might be a little blurry on, and second, this is a valuable opportunity to connect with someone you may well need in your corner later. Talk to them about your project, get them on board early and make them feel important. You'll hear (read) me say this again but seize all these little opportunities to connect in person with those involved in, and affected by, your business change agenda. Get out there and show yourself. Get other supporters of your project to reveal themselves too. Stand up and be counted.

The Organisational Chart

This flowchart is the official outline of how your organisation works – a formal structure that registers everyone in every division and department, illustrates their relative position and responsibilities in the hierarchy, and indicates who they report to; it is not exactly rocket science. It's something that you've seen a hundred times before, so it shouldn't send you running for the hills.

This exercise may or may not be necessary for you, depending on what groundwork has already been done in your organisation. Now is probably a really good time to stop by Neela in HR to see if someone has already invested time in outlining the hierarchy, so you can work with what's already there. If you can get your hands on a readymade Organisational Chart, great. Make sure you check it thoroughly and update it if necessary, so you don't end up including people who left your organisation ages ago.

If there's no existing Organisational Chart to be found anywhere, let's get to work. Here are the instructions to generate your flowchart:

1. Begin by recording all the corporate divisions in your organisation in columns.

2. Then add the departments within those divisions in a row beneath, with the individual teams within those departments sitting below that.

3. Now identify who leads each section, working from the C-level managers, directors and senior managers, down to middle managers and team leaders.

4. List all other employees in their respective roles and ranks.

5. Draw lines between people to indicate their formal relationships.

6. Try to look beyond the official structures to become attuned to relationships and interactions which could have an impact on your project, if your company is split between on- and off-site working arrangements, or if your project involves and affects people from several different locations. Don't forget to mark who works from where.

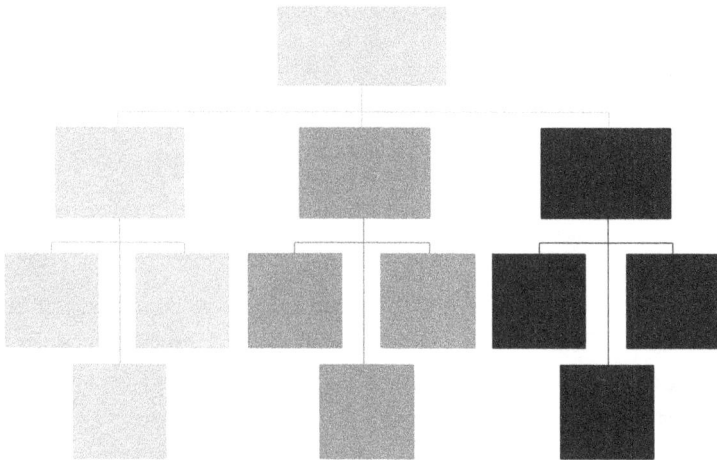

A blank organisational chart

Just a couple of small tips:

- There are hundreds of different types of organisational charts and yours could use any one of them. If you have to generate one from scratch, you could always use one of the many online tools designed to help people visualise their organisational structure, to save precious time and protect your sanity.

- Use colours and fancy shapes to your heart's content. Or at least to whatever extent is useful to help you navigate your chart if it's getting increasingly big and complicated.

CASE STUDY: RIVER CONSTRUCTION

Allow me to introduce you to River Construction, an imaginary company that we will return to throughout this book. I will describe how I would work as a change manager within River Construction, with the aim of demonstrating how all the activities can work through a life cycle of a single project within our fictional organisation. For simplicity, I will draw all my examples from here, but rest assured, the BEE Methodology will work with any type of company, of any size and in any industry.

River
Construction.

Logo for our fictional case study company, River Construction

River Construction is a global construction firm, working across fifty countries worldwide, with 11,000 colleagues, and touching the lives of millions by providing the skills needed to build economies and grow societies. It is planning to introduce Microsoft 365 (M365), an online productivity platform, to its teams, but there are significant complexities within the company, with business units working across various countries, and teams reporting into different management lines. Thankfully River Construction already has several shared services in use, including in L&D and Communications (Comms), but the organisation is at a low level of change maturity.

This change project's focus was the roll out of the M365 suite across the business to create a modern digital workplace. This involved the adoption and reinforcement of ten specific components of M365, split across two different phases: a mass adoption of the community tools, and a targeted adoption of the content and collaboration tools.

Executive summary

The aim is to provide River Construction colleagues with two things, selected M365 tools and an adoption strategy by which all colleagues can gain access and insight into M365, its products and features, as well as understanding how it can solve their challenges. An additional aim is to encourage behavioural change and adoption of the products.

This change project therefore comprises the following phases:

- **Discovery phase**

- **Phase 1:** Community tools: Yammer, Microsoft To Do and Microsoft Whiteboard

- **Phase 2:** Content and collaboration tools: Microsoft Planner, SharePoint Online, Microsoft Forms and Microsoft Teams

  This phase has been further broken down into:

  − Alpha

  − Beta

  − Full roll out

Project benefits

As part of the Discovery phase, it was revealed that River Construction lacked tools to enable open and engaged teams and communities to form and collaborate efficiently, which was leading to poor performance and productivity across the group. By adopting M365, River Construction will gain the following benefits:

- Fit-for-purpose products
- 'Best in show' productivity tools
- Use of a world-class secure platform

- Improved engagement

- Clearer communication channels

- An open network

- An inclusive area for feedback, updates and questions

- Enhanced time saving

As the change manager at the fictional River Construction, I sent out my Organisation Assessment and from this one questionnaire I learned a lot about the organisation. The first part of the questionnaire provided me with the information about who the person was, their department, job title and who they reported to.

Organisational Chart for River Construction

While I could have done this next stage manually, I chose instead to put it through my BEE Insights tool. This generated the data I needed to create the Organisational Chart for River Construction.

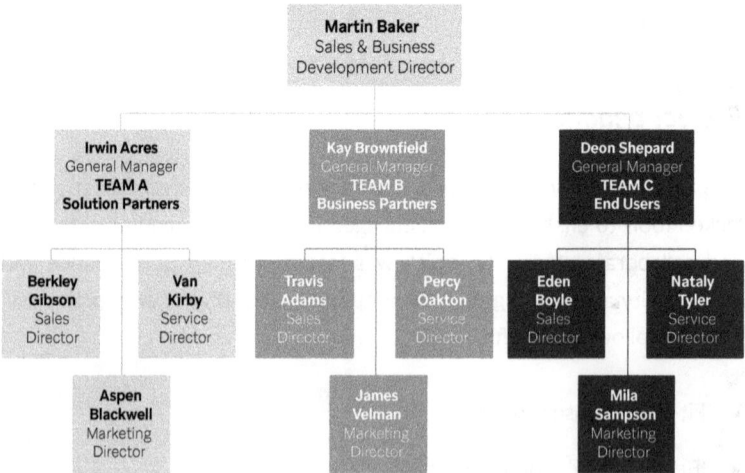

Organisational Chart for a single department within River Construction

Using this Organisational Chart, I can quickly determine the levels of seniority within the company. This provides me with a clear understanding of where, and with whom, I need to begin my engagement conversations (but more of that coming soon).

Never underestimate the power of personal assistants. Some one-to-one sessions with this group of players will ensure the widespread distribution of, and advocacy for, both your project and training.

The Organisation Assessment

Over the years, I have identified five areas that clearly determine whether your business change project is getting off to a good start or is doomed from the beginning. You will probably agree that it's important to understand your organisation's approaches to change, technology, communication and training before you can go about introducing more change, technology, communication and training, right?

The five areas that determine change success are:

1. **Change readiness:** how your organisation generally performs in times of change based on people's ease with how changes are managed and implemented. The more change ready an organisation is, the better its understanding regarding the importance of change and its level of impact.

2. **Confidence with technology:** how people view new technologies and how comfortable they feel about it in comparison to the rest of their team. Every organisation contains individuals with wide ranging levels of confidence, experience and expertise with using technology.

Understanding this will highlight how focused your training and engagement needs to be; the more confident people are, the shorter and more focused you can make it.

3. **Communications:** how people are engaged versus how they would like to be, and how channels of communication engage different people. Understanding how the organisation uses communication methods and technologies will help you generate the best engagement plans, ensuring communication is targeting and received by the largest audience. Remember, word of mouth is incredibly powerful: if most of your people tend to communicate through, say, the intranet, lean on this and let those people spread the word to the others.

4. **Potential impact:** how big of a disruption your project is going to be to people and whether they might resist the change. How work-/life-changing will this be to people? If it is likely to cause significant impact and disturbance, then, *no-brainer*, a lot more change management will be required.

5. **Training preferences:** how people like to learn. There is no point shoving colleagues into online training if they aren't going to attend. Know your audience, and know how they want to learn.

This is a whole lot to find out and learn, but don't worry – I've prepared a set of questions for each of the categories that you can easily import into a simple questionnaire or suitable software.

These are your next steps:

1. Answer the questions using our online form, or use the Organisation Assessment available in BEE Insights.

2. Start sending it out to everyone involved in or affected by the business change. Ensure you include a clear deadline – you can't wait forever.

3. Collate the data, or allow BEE Insights to pull it together automatically.

4. Analyse the data; remember to lean on your business analysts to help with this or use our how-to-work-the-data guidelines.

5. Use this data to inform your business change strategy as you move forward.

PDF of Organisation Assessment   BEE Insights tool

CASE STUDY: RIVER CONSTRUCTION

Let us consider these five areas that determine change success in relation to our fictional company. I've already mentioned that River Construction is a complex international organisation operating across eight global regions. Any change project that is to succeed, despite significant regional differences, and a high degree of diversity among the workforce, would therefore need substantial support from the organisational structures.

To complete the Organisation Assessment, I was supported by the corporate Comms department, who had excellent access to the regional and local teams. These teams distributed the questionnaires to a total of 500 people, and on analysing the results, I made the following observations.

1. Change readiness

River Construction was not comfortable with the overall amount of technology changes happening across the organisation. There was felt to be a lack of consistency and worryingly low levels of support, with poor communication and inadequate training about the change. To address this, during our Build phase I was able to coach the head of technology, recommending that more structured steps should be introduced to result in an improved change approach within their projects. For my change project, I ensured a strong brand identity and planned consistent messaging across everything I communicated to the business.

2. Confidence with technology

The results were divided: many of the demographic felt confident with technology, but there was also a significant group of people that felt relatively unskilled and lacked confidence. It was also apparent from the results that most staff didn't feel that they were given enough time for training and learning.

To address this, I proposed leaning on the more confident people among the group by increasing the size of the planned champion network, to ensure plenty of peer support for those who felt less competent. The concerns around time provided for training and consolidation of learning were reported back to the head of HR for additional focus and to consider changes to processes and policies as part of a company-wide review.

3. Communications

It was immediately clear from the results that River Construction has a strong communications focus and a large majority of their people made use of all channels available to them; however, there was one strong winner in terms of communication preference, and this was face-to-face.

It was therefore crucial to ensure that I focused lots on the engagement of the influencers and the support provided to the senior management team, to ensure the delivery of regular updates to the teams through their meetings and one-to-one catch-up sessions. I drew up a calendar to understand when each business unit hosted their team meetings and ensured the project had a presence at each of these meetings.

4. Impact

The results revealed an anticipated high degree of impact on their current ways of working; respondents also indicated a lack of understanding about how they would be supported through the change. Based on these results, it was clearly important to increase the support and training offered for the project, but the most important step was to encourage the support teams to become part of the project working group. This ensured a smooth handover once a business unit was onboarded to the new system.

5. Training preferences

What a shocking result this was. To support the claims made about training preferences and time given to learn, respondents were asked to indicate their awareness of and frequency of attendance at any training offered. The majority of those surveyed felt unsupported with training, had never attended it or didn't know it was there. The best way to tackle this was to make training mandatory for specific parts of the system, for example the security and data risk elements. Training was also provided in an easy-to-learn format (broken down to make it more digestible) and the L&D team was engaged to build the training into the learning management system and mark it as mandatory. The board of directors provided a top-down directive on the mandatory modules.

7

PEOPLE

CHANGE IS BOTH SCIENCE AND ART

You may be thinking that your mission here is simple: just to quickly plan and deliver an improvement, restructure some part of your organisation's operations, revamp and modify a rather vintage system or a couple of outdated processes, or tweak the hierarchy a little. Perhaps you find yourself using these words to describe your project: 'quickly', 'just', 'a little'... You may think it's no big deal, but you couldn't be more wrong.

What you're really doing here is completely suspending people's routines, pulling apart their teams and departments workflows, and disrupting the way things are done – and have always been done – at your organisation. You are throwing a huge spanner deep into the works. I know that sounds a bit harsh, and it is not meant to make you feel like some sort of crazed anarchist, but it is the reality of the situation. By moving forward with your business change agenda, you are not just introducing a little and insignificant change, unnoticed by some; rather you are cutting a deep incision into the everyday operations of the business, and forcing people to adapt.

Change challenges people's prefrontal cortex to develop and adopt completely novel ways of thinking and behaving, and that takes some serious brain science.

In this chapter, I'll look at how people experience change, from a neuroscientific and psychological perspective. Understanding this will leave you better equipped to understand and deal with their reactions to your change project.

You're not training to be a neurosurgeon (or, probably you're not...), but you're about to gain a little neuro-insight.

The neuroscience of change (Part I)

Neuroscience is concerned with the structure and function of the nervous system and its relation to behaviour and learning.[16,17] Among other things, it explores how a person feels, thinks and acts and why.

In the context of any kind of change, personal or professional, neuroscience can explain people's natural aversion to difference and the inherent discomfort we feel in the presence of uncertainty. There are a huge number of explanations and theories to explain this, but – I'll keep it extremely brief here – fundamentally they all boil down to an instinctive and evolutionary urge to assure survival, such as by maintaining a certain social status (because having nobody out in the wild, hunting for your means to survive, simply doesn't work) or by preserving a degree of autonomy and self-determination.[18] I know that I simply like constancy: for things to be, and stay, as I know them to be.

Change is the opposite of the patterns of cohesion that our brains naturally seek safety in.

Individual experiences of business change

While we're no longer in the Stone Age and people don't fear for their lives and limbs in the workplace, they may still fear for their livelihoods.

Change induces a fear of loss and inhibition, and it poses a serious threat to people.

To proactively address this fear, there are a number of key steps that should be followed when introducing your change project. It is important to acknowledge these natural emotions towards change, stimulate positive thoughts on difference, and encourage forward-looking thinking and action. You should seize the opportunity this presents to get to better understand each person who will be affected by your business change project and identify where their difficulties lie. In other words, go and talk to your people. Not just Alex from PR or Kim from Marketing whose help you'll need with the project, but also talk to Charlie and Vic from Accounts, who will have to figure out a new way of working. Talking to these individuals now, during the Build phase, allows you to address their individual concerns and issues, and also come to understand how best to support them further down the road when working through the Excite and Equip phases.

Have you ever heard of our brains described as 'a social organ'?[19] Or of humans as 'meaning-making machines'?[20] Well, now you're about to find out what these mean.

Business change and the collective dynamic

The problem that you're about to face is that the behaviour you're trying to modify is not just confined to one person's brain, nor is it just a collection of individual difficulties; that would be far too easy. Instead, the behaviour of those you're about to disrupt is firmly embedded in the social fabric of your organisation that has developed its own dynamics and currents over time. It is entwined in the existing ways of working and woven into the narratives that have been constructed by the people, teams and departments within your organisation that keep things going.

That is why I argue that we must also look at your organisation as a collection of social clusters and a network of interpersonal relationships and communication channels. It might have dawned on you already, but an organisation exists not in its computers and cloud technologies, nor even in its accumulation of individuals, but in the spaces and connections between.

To get a better sense of the entanglement, we're going to perform a Key Stakeholder Engagement Evaluation. This will help us understand the various ways your project is perceived within the organisation, based on the answers of a select group of people. We'll then move on to creating the most delicate 'Who's Who' of it all: a Social Network Analysis that visualises all the nodes (the individual players) and connections (their relationships and interactions) that together make up the social fabric of the place. This is where you find the right people to support the change. I suggest you go and get warmed up: this is the part where you will strategically position your pieces on the chessboard and get ready to attack.

> Businesses are made up of their people, and it's the connective tissue that matters here – the social glue that creates the organisation.

Oh, one last thing: 'neuroscience has discovered that the brain is super plastic. Even the most entrenched behaviors can be modified.'[21] This is hugely encouraging: no matter how resistant people may initially seem towards your proposed change, science tells you that they are capable of adapting.

Summary

In any change project, it's critical to bring the people with you. To do this, it is imperative that you look into the emotions, thoughts and actions of the individuals involved. Without wanting to spoil your discovery, inevitably you will find that they are influenced by those who surround them and by the commonly told narratives and behavioural patterns within your organisation.

An organisation exists in the relationships that those individuals cultivate with one another, in their interactions and in how they – together – engage with the rest of the world. To uncover these relationships, you can use two key tools: my Key Stakeholder Engagement Evaluation, and the Social Network Analysis, which is how you'll uncover your secret weapons, your champions and influencers.

8

EXERCISES: PEOPLE
THE PEOPLE TOOLS

Uncovering the networks of motivation and influence in your organisation is tricky but I have two tools that make it easier: the Key Stakeholder Engagement Evaluation and the Social Network Analysis.

The Key Stakeholder Engagement Evaluation

Not everyone in your organisation is immediately going to think, feel and act exactly as you'd like them to think, feel and act. Some of them don't even fully understand what the heck is going on with this project that you keep talking about. Every person in your organisation is in a different place when it comes to engaging with the fancy new ways of working that you're keen to introduce, and you are going to have to find out how to work with all of these.

While you're mulling over the results of the Organisation Assessment, send out this quick Key Stakeholder Engagement Evaluation questionnaire to the people who will be impacted by the change – start with those you already know as key stakeholders. If you're still unsure, a good place to start would be with your senior management, your project sponsor and anyone holding a prominent position, as indicated in your Organisational Chart.

The Key Stakeholder Engagement Evaluation exercise is about systematically discovering and plotting people's understanding of your project. I suggest you consider this in relation to five general areas that together indicate the level of engagement with the change:

1. **Project knowledge:** what people already know about the objectives and aims of your project.

2. **Time available for project:** how much time people will realistically be able to invest in the change to help themselves and others adopt the project and adapt.

3. **Communication preferences:** how and where people like to be kept informed about what's going on.

4. **Project alignment:** how well people think your project fits into the general strategy and existing processes, and how well they think you will manage the project.

5. **Perceived project importance:** how people's individual goals and objectives link to the project and whether they consider it one of their personal priorities.

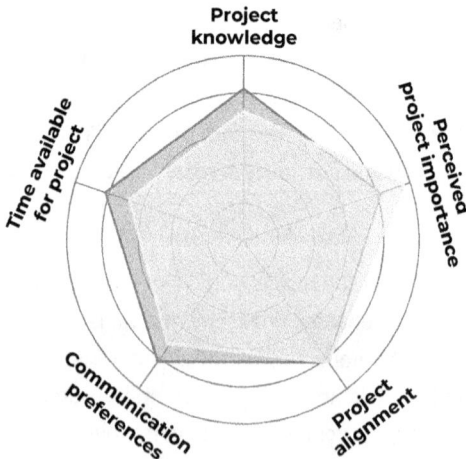

Results (overlaid) from two stakeholders across the five areas of engagement

Here's how to go about this exercise:

1. Transfer our questions into a suitable online tool.

2. Send it out to your key stakeholders; ensure you include a clear deadline – you can't wait forever.

3. Pull the data together.

4. Analyse the data with a view to what you want your key stakeholders to know and how to think.

5. Use this data to inform your business change strategy.

Don't forget: if you wish to make it easier, you can use the Key Stakeholder Engagement Evaluation tool available through BEE Insights.

PDF to Key Stakeholder
Engagement Evaluation:

BEE Insights tool:

What is a business change strategy?

A business change strategy is similar to a project plan, providing all involved with guidance on exactly how you will prepare for and implement the change. It should align with the existing project plans, including the timelines, cost and resources.

CASE STUDY: RIVER CONSTRUCTION

I know already from my previous work on River Construction that it has a diverse membership. With up to five generations in the workplace for the first time in history and staff working across many countries with significantly different cultures and attitudes, it's particularly important to understand how on board the stakeholders are to the project.[22]

The company's Organisational Chart showed an unambiguous traditional management hierarchy. The project team therefore assumed that approval of the business change would follow the same top-down structure, and identified the senior executive partner as their most important key stakeholder. However, when the results of the Key Stakeholder Engagement Evaluation were analysed, the director's questionnaire revealed significant indifference towards the project and a brutal lack of knowledge about its mission; this was a red flag in the system. The results for the other key stakeholders revealed varying degrees of project understanding and ability to communicate and advocate the change, with a significant number who were currently showing little awareness of or willingness to engage with the project. These were immediate areas of alarm and therefore these were the first people to tackle and bring more on board.

Knowing better than to be disappointed by the results, the project team next looked at the results from the Key Stakeholder Engagement Evaluation in conjunction with the Organisational Chart; they also considered the Corporate Survey that documented the current growth spurt. By considering these results together, they realised that the senior management was too busy developing and growing their business to get involved in a business change project that was being led by a team whose working approach they had to trust because it was so far removed from their usual management style. Even better, on studying the overlap of chart and evaluation again, it became apparent that the senior partner's direct report was well informed and supportive of the business change project. This was a green flag in the system – an individual who would communicate

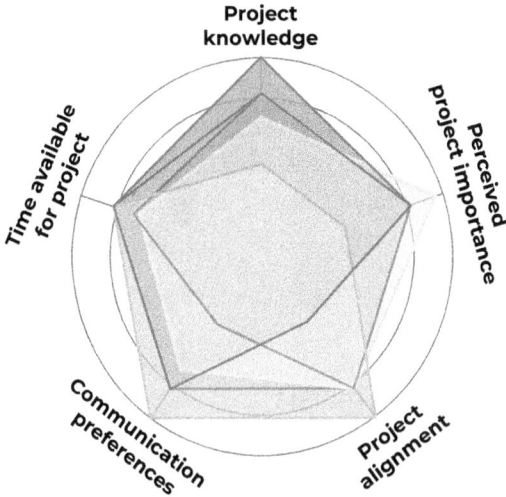

Engagement results (overlaid) from several key stakeholders in River Construction

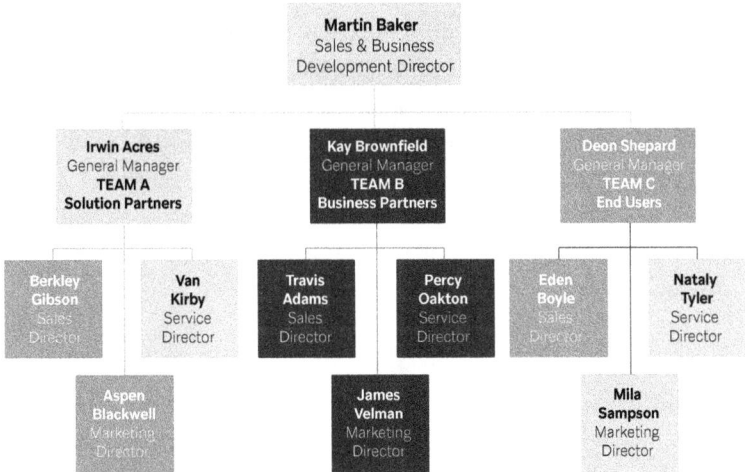

Organisational Chart demonstrating the potential impact if Kay Brownfield, a key stakeholder at River Construction, becomes disengaged. Rectifying this by focusing attention on her is also likely to re-engage all those reporting into her.

relevant updates to the senior partner in a language and manner that the they would understand.

This leads us to another golden rule: the data sets collected during the Build phase should always be considered in conjunction with one another. This process of combining and cross-checking is called sense-making, and I think the reason why is obvious.

Social Network Analysis

I've already been pretty clear on this subject: an organisation exists in its people, their relationships and interactions with one another. An organisation *is* its people, and that is why the Social Network Analysis is one of the most powerful analysis exercises you'll do in the Build phase.

There is nothing more important for you to know than who is talking to whom at the meeting table or in the break room, and who will listen to whom when push comes to shove. Consider this the unofficial version of the Organisational Chart, the informal response network within your organisation, the chart of truth that tells you how things really work. Who is the social ringleader and who is the person everyone goes to with their technical problems? Don't you want to know who can help you with this work? I am about to introduce you to what is essentially the science of how to find that person.

Get ready to see a visual representation of the individual players and their relationships and interactions, a colour-coded visualisation of the social web that fills your organisation and that you experience every single day. From this, you'll be able to identify your change agents, the champions and influencers: the people that others go to for help, those who have immense influence on the overall moods and attitudes within the business, and the people who know just about everything that's going on within your organisation.

A 'change champion' ('champion' from now on) is the person who others trust and confide in when they have technical problems. A champion is a natural encourager and promoter with a proactive mindset, always enthusiastic and keen to understand the technicalities and details of new initiatives and technologies. They are usually good communicators, with a high social currency, so strong leadership and training skills, and ability to do peer coaching. They are always happy to help, but they're the kind of people who would first put their own face mask on and then turn to help others in the case of cabin pressure loss on an aeroplane.

A 'change influencer' ('influencer') is the person others turn to for emotional support and to whom you turn to fine-tune your approach to business change. They are a strong-willed and persuasive person who sets the mood and directs the responses of others, giving a voice to the change while still

Remember to look back to your Organisational Chart to understand where your champions and influencers sit in the organisation and who they can influence.

being mindful of others and making time to listen to their problems. They understand the importance of the champions in the process and fully support their work by communicating up and down the hierarchy.

Follow these simple instructions to map your own network:

1. Carry out a Social Network Analysis. The easiest way is to use a data analytic tool; use BEE Insights if you wish.

2. Alternatively, send a quick questionnaire round your people that enquires about their social habits at work.

3. Gather and process the data, then create a clear but comprehensive visualisation of the social fabric of the organisation.

4. Take a really good look at the results, taking as much time as you need.

5. Research the people found in the epicentre of the social interaction web.

Build, Excite, Equip.

PDF to Social Network Analysis: BEE Insights tool:

A good data analysis will provide you with a social network analysis chart that looks like this:

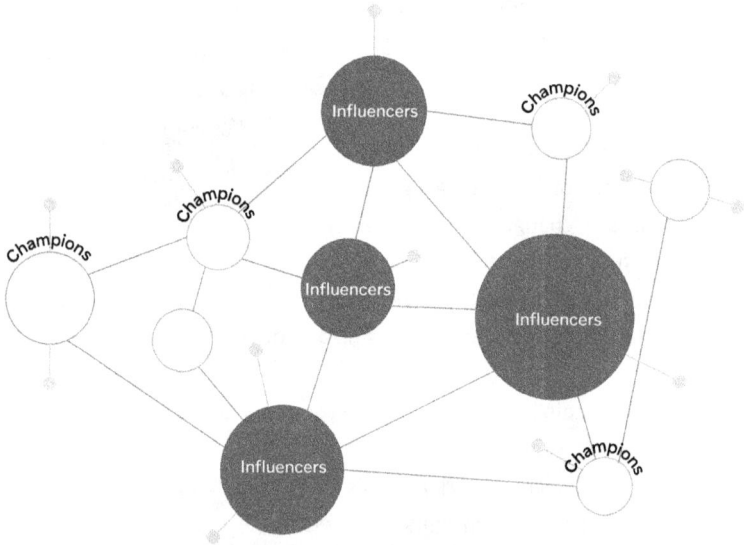

CASE STUDY: RIVER CONSTRUCTION

Ensuring that I created a good network of influencers and champions across River Construction was crucial to deploying M365 successfully. After all, I needed to have influencers advocating for the change and helping to scale the communications effectively. Our in-depth Social Network Analysis of the company provided us with some interesting insights.

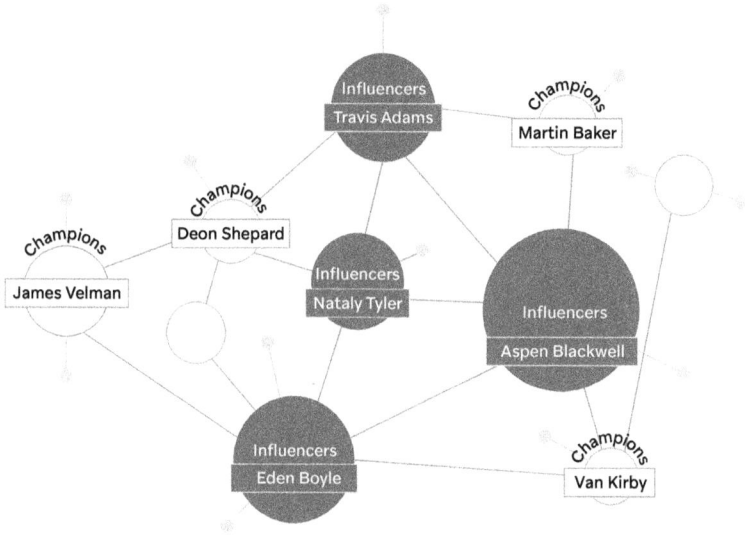

A visualisation of the champions and influencers at River Construction

Coming to understand this unofficial organisation of support across the company significantly influenced the approach chosen for the rolling out of the new tool. By identifying the influencers and champions, I was able to establish who to train first and where to turn for insight into people's actual feelings and progress in the transition phase – not to mention who to pat on the shoulder for a business change well facilitated. The three-stage roll out plan suddenly seemed much less intimidating, knowing that there was already an organic support system among the large group of researchers.

Our next golden rule: never extrapolate from what you would do to assume that others would do the same, it's simply not how the world works.

9

PROJECT

THE REAL CONCERN

Now that you've had a good look around your organisation and come to understand both its fabric and structure (with its general setup and its special quirks) and also its people (their overall moods and perceptions, their relationships and interactions, and how they're warming up to your business change agenda), it's time to put your own house in order.

In this chapter, we will look at project planning: your project management plan, schedule, project objectives, key performance indicators (KPIs) and action plans.

With your business change project, you're leading a lot of people across unknown territories, and to many of them, that might feel something like a night-time walk, through the wetlands, with one broken flashlight and no rubber boots.

If you're going to cause disruption and disarray with the introduction of your project, do it with a sense of responsibility and absolute clarity of purpose, so that nobody gets lost in the dark. I feel better about any business change approached in this manner, and I promise you will too.

This part of the Build phase is a bit of a 'return to the self' journey (minus the philosophical jabbering), and so we need a 'business change packing list for project managers', so to speak. We need to make sure that you know the reality of your project and have everything prepared to really dive in and make a difference. Remember, everyone's sanity is at stake and that should account for something. That is precisely why we're now going to poke around your project a bit.

Establishing the basics

Question 1 (at the risk of overstepping...): Do you have a bulletproof project management plan that you can cling to once you step into the ring?

(You know, one that covers the full scope of the project, defines the deliverables in enough detail, documents the availability of resources, states the overall budget, considers timings/the timeline/time available, and so on and so forth...?)

I'm sure that you've already covered all this and I certainly don't want to undermine or appear to be questioning your expertise and progress; after all, that plan was probably instrumental in securing funding for this project and in getting permission to overthrow people's work routines (aka obtaining the licence required to take them on that night-time walk through the wetlands). However, as important as having a fantastic project management plan in the first place, is to keep updating it on a regular basis. This is how you'll integrate your project management plan with your business change management plan and keep everything on track.

In theory, it'll then look something like the following flowchart.

In practice, it's more complex than it now appears, but it's good to get the general idea.

Project Gantt chart

Task	MARCH				APRIL				MAY				JUNE				JULY				AUGUST			
	10	11	12	13	14	15	16	17	18	19	20	21	22	23	24	25	26	27	28	29	30	31	32	33
Identify																								
Define the business case		■																						
Align to business benefits			■	■																				
Plan																								
Develop stakeholder engagement plans					■	■																		
Understand change impacts						■	■																	
Define success criteria							■	■																
Delivery																								
Manage operational change									■	■	■													
Communications and training plan									■	■														
Create operating plans and procedures											■	■												
Go live																								
Go live checklist													■											
Go live support													■	■	■	■								
Handover																								
BAU process																	■	■						
Transfer responsibility to the owner																			■	■				
Project close																								
Explore lessons learned																					■	■		
Project closure document																					■	■	■	
Celebrate project success																							■	■

Know your purpose

Question 2: What is the underlying reason for your business change (aka why are you and your people on a night-time walk through the wetlands)?

Your project surely intends to help people do their best work and make things easier per your definition of working practice, but can you readily and simply explain that to someone who's not so sure about the whole thing?

The kind of message that we're looking for is one that is top of mind, always at your fingertips, even at three o'clock in the morning when thinking is hard and your eyes won't open. Your answer should be available to draw on without a moment's thought, anywhere, anytime.

Your business change project is an intentional strategic initiative that is meaningful to your organisation's overall vision and its achievement. *It really matters, a whole gigantic lot.* That is why you must be fully in touch with your project's purpose and its reason for existence, and share it to your heart's content. While it will disrupt people's current working practices (and yes, there's no doubt that's hard), it is also a striving for progress and therefore deserves a proper mission statement. Connecting your project's purpose and people's benefits makes sense.

Define and track success

The best mission statement in the world won't be any help if you have no idea where you're headed. Remember, if even you don't know where this business change is going, imagine just how clueless and confused your fellow wayfarers will be feeling, wandering aimlessly through the night with wet feet.

Question 3: What is it that you expect people to be able to do at the end of all this?

It's of the utmost importance (I repeat: utmost importance, exclamation mark!) that you have first defined the future you're aiming for, if you are to be able to recognise when you've reached your destination. To do this, you need to create a Successful Adoption Definition, outlined in a small number of criteria that specify precisely what behaviour is required of people if you are to consider them full adopters of your business change. Picture the grand finish lines at the end of marathons – London, New York, Berlin – and the unmistakable flair of accomplishment that surrounds them; you need to replicate this here, so have a think about how.

Once you have identified what you will consider a successful adoption, decide and prepare how you will track people's progress; what good is it to know where people need to go without being able to measure whether they're actually getting there?

You therefore need to look more closely at people's user behaviour with the new product or process, their willingness to change their existing working routines, and their knowledge in applying it to generate new working routines. In other words, you need to track people's adoption progress, their awareness of its benefits, and levels of user confidence. Would you believe it? I happen to have another exercise ready for you – the ABC Scorecard. This will quickly become your best friend and success measure, and will be considered in more detail in Chapter 10, when we consider how we will define and measure our success.

Formulating action plans

It's time to step up your game from taking inventory to talking strategy. You should have completed, or gotten close to completing, your Build plans, outlining your organisation, your people and now also your project. You should have a rough idea of how things work, who is who and where you're going.

In my humble experience, project managers and their teams are generally extremely good at formulating action plans, or more specifically, the communication and training plans, so I'm just going to highlight quickly what you should consider when using the BEE Methodology. If it hasn't yet clicked, your communication plan – or, as I prefer to call it, the engagement plan – refers largely to what happens during the Excite phase, in which you'll be creating communication aids, connecting with stakeholders and marketing your project. Your

> *The remaining question is: what needs to happen to get everyone to the finish line? That, dear friend, will be clarified in your first set of action plans. Things are moving forward.*

training plans refer predominantly to the Equip phase and everything related to developing learning materials, coaching everyone according to their individual needs and invigorating your project with success-related content. I therefore suggest that you start strategising, planning actions and continuously revising and improving them as you read through the next chapters in this book.

Engagement planning

More often than not, I've witnessed communication plans being drawn up by a project team, and the main focus of this communication tends to be tactical communications: T-10 anyone? As you'll see when you reach the 'Getting the word out: rethinking communication' section (see Chapter 11), communication is about so much more than simply emails or tactical communications. Communication is all about engagement. Its power lies in engaging in a way that resonates with the audience, tapping into their psyche so that they pay attention to what you are trying to say.

Powerful communication matters: only 20% of colleagues will read an email sent from a project team, whereas 80% of colleagues will read one from their line manager. Furthermore,[23] 'only 7% of our communication is verbal – the content of our communication. 38% is conveyed through the quality of voice – tone, volume, speed and pitch. 55% is through posture, movements, gestures, facial expressions, breathing and skin-color changes.'[24] *Pretty shocking statistics, huh?* It is clear that if you want your stakeholders to read your news updates, you need to start thinking about some pretty interesting and clever ways to engage them: team meetings, town halls, roadshows, social networks and so on.

For now, this is just the start of engagement planning, so let's begin something during Build and continue to develop it as we go along, as you would your project initiation documentation (PID). The best way to create interesting engagement plans is to dive deep into the information needs of the business. The best and simplest way to do this is – *ready for it?* – to ask them. Ask the people how, when, what and who they honestly listen to within the company. We have a communications assessment as part of our BEE Insights tool that will send surveys out asking about this, but it's as easy to create one by following these simple steps:

1. **Speak to shared services.** How are the teams in HR, L&D, Comms, IT and Marketing all communicating? They will know about the existing town halls, company events and communication channels. Lean on them and ask them these questions.

2. **Ask the heads of departments.** When you are engaging with senior leadership teams, ask them about their management meetings, and if you're feeling confident, get an early commitment from them to discuss it with their teams.

3. **Question the people.** Ask them what existing communication channels they read and make use of, and what are their preferences; this will guide where you should best spend your time. If everyone suggests that their preference is the company newsletter, then get ready to smooth talk the editor or content creator and start planning to include your communication information in the newsletter. Cake always helps.

Communication Assessments:

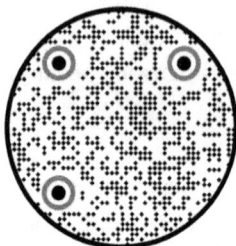

Training planning

Training plans should be created with a clear understanding of what the people need from their training. For example, for an organisation with a large number of remote workers, it is quite unrealistic to expect them to attend on-site training, just as it is to ask an organisation with a larger older generation of colleagues to receive training just by viewing quick videos. Knowing your audience is vital to this and the Comms teams are your trump card here. We have a training assessment in BEE Insights that asks people their preferred ways of learnings, but this is something you can start to plan here and evolve over the project as you speak to more and more people.

Training Assessments:

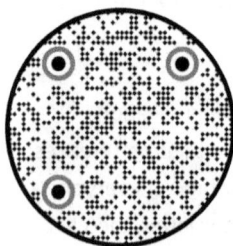

The art of timing: It's not now or never

You might now be feeling an irresistible urge to dig in and get started – an insistent desire to turn things upside down, schedule lots of meetings and start getting the word out. It's important to get to grips with the urgency of the situation and put on that proactive mindset, because you're really going to need that kind of energy for the days (and weeks, and months...) ahead as the changes take place.

While there are some great stories of impulsive audacious deeds, with great results matched by their sensational now-or-never flavour, you might want to have a look at the calendar first. *Calendars, in fact.* Your industry-specific calendar, which gives you an idea what is happening in the grander scheme of things; your organisation-specific calendar, which shows you exactly what structure governs the internal annual cycle; and your project-specific calendar, which lets you check in with your own working reality. You'll also want to have a look at a people-specific calendar to see what everyone you're really counting on in this process is up to and when. You can't possibly consider every single doctor's appointment and every request for paternal leave, but to co-ordinate your timeline with that of the key influencers and those who have a significant impact on the moods and perceptions of the pack is crucial to the successful delivery of your project.

Here's a scenario: imagine that Frankie from the in-house canteen (a popular social hub) is away on a three-week vacation at the same time as you're trying to roll out the biggest business change in the company's history. The result is stress on all levels, anxiety and discontent hanging in the air, no comfort food around and an absence of the daily ritual of sitting together for an hour at lunch each day – the one truly accessible setting in the building, where honest conversations are held, support is offered and sought out, and companionship is found.

This is a small anecdote just to get you thinking that there might be people in your organisation who hold the gang together more genuinely and effectively than any officially appointed well-being manager ever could.

Summary

For project managers, this may be familiar ground but it doesn't mean you can skip this step of project planning. You need to define your purpose and be clear on how to recognise success as well as how you will be tracking your progress toward it. You need to formulate your action plan, ensure the schedule is realistic and that the key people – whether it's senior management or Frankie in the canteen – are all available to provide support.

10

EXERCISES: PROJECT
THE PROJECT TOOLS

I'm sure you'll agree that planning is critical to the success of any project, so here I'll be sharing my change management project tips and tools to help you set up your mission statement, Successful Adoption Definition, and Adoption Success Rating, and determine the ideal scheduling.

Mission statement

Clearly defining the rationale of your project helps generate organic buy-in from the people in your organisation who are affected by and involved in the business change. It sets out to describe the purpose of it all – the 'What will be accomplished?' and 'What do I get out of it?' Having a ready answer to those questions will help direct many a conversation in the future.

While having a clear mission statement allows you to get the message out to the people successfully and succinctly, it also allows you (and your incredible project team) to really drill into the fundamental purpose of the whole endeavour. Articulating your mission can help you wrap your own head around the project and saying it out loud (and possibly being challenged in response) may be your vehicle to truly internalising that message in the Build phase and then branding your project in the later Excite phase. Try not to go down a marketing rabbit hole and extending this into a ten-week brain-busting exercise. Get to grips with your project's rationale by exploring the reason for its existence, the desired accomplishments and the benefits it'll ultimately bring to people.

A few tips for writing your mission statement:

1. Stick to plain English; keep the language and sentence structure simple.

2. Keep the message clear and concise.

3. Don't over-formalise the process; scribble on some scrap paper if you wish.

Here's an example of a good mission statement, because writing one can seem a truly onerous task: 'Our mission is to connect teams and departments across countries and continents for seamless workflows and international collaboration.'

Successful Adoption Definition

Somehow you must find a way to capture where you're going with your business change project, and to specify when exactly your mission can be considered fully accomplished. There's a certain kind of behaviour that you expect everyone in your organisation to have adopted if you are to cross the finish line, and this is the time to draw the figurative mark on the ground, via your Successful Adoption Definition.

This definition is relevant to the successful delivery of your project in more ways than one: as much as you're interested in determining whether individual people have fully adopted the prescribed changes, the people affected by and involved in the business change will also want to know what is expected of them and know how to track where in the adoption journey they are. Defining your success criteria will help you establish these expectations and make progress in the adoption journey visible. One way to go about this is to ask yourself the question: 'What should the new status quo look like in X department/Y team/Z workflow?'

While I like absolute answers in uncertain situations, I'm afraid there simply isn't one specific way of defining what a successful adoption looks like, nor could I – or should I – seek to describe success for your change project. You must consider what you generally want people's future user behaviour, product or process understanding, and work experience to be; by doing this, you're already laying the foundation for the next exercise.

Think about your key audience who will be impacted by the change? What will be the differences in what you are saying, doing, feeling and thinking as a result of a successful change?

Adoption Success Rating

You knew there would have to be some KPIs eventually. We've all been waiting for this moment as it releases us from the anxiety of not having tangible measures to report to project sponsors, C-level managers, Her Majesty the Queen and whoever else would like to know what's going on and where their money is going.

The ABC Scorecard is the BEE-specific success rating that helps you understand how close you are getting to being able to announce a successful change adoption. Participating in this survey is obligatory for everyone who

ABC Scorecard.

is affected by the business change – this is nonnegotiable – and the results are your indication of whether or not people are coming around to the new status quo. Because the scorecard captures people's progress along their individual change journeys, this exercise is done at least twice: definitely once before initiation (Build phase or Excite phase) and once after coaching

(Equip phase), plus, if necessary, a third time after having rerun the Coach and/or Invigorate stages.

The ABC Scorecard is an acronym:

A = Adoption

B = Be Aware

C = Competence

The results you'll get from this rating will look something like this:

A: for someone who is frequently using the product, talking about it and willing to integrate it into their workflows

B: for someone who is familiar with the product's features, understands their benefits and is excited about using them to make their working lives easier

C: for someone who is comfortable in using the product on an everyday basis

The survey's questions are divided into the three categories: Adoption, Be Aware, Competence; the respondent's answers to these questions are rated 1–5, the higher the rating, the stronger they are in that specific area. The aim of this scoring is to ensure that the individual has improved in each of the three areas by the end of the engagement. Regularly measuring this allows you (or the champions that you're putting in to lead their colleagues) to assess individuals' development and ensure they have the correct support that they need during the adoption plan.

It is likely that you will see results heavily weighted in one or two areas, like the following example, from an individual who scores particularly highly in adoption and awareness:

AB: for someone who is:

frequently using the product, talking about it and integrating it in their workflows

+

familiar with product features and excited about using them to make their working lives easier

Your aim is to get everyone to achieve good scores in all three areas:

ABC: for someone who is:

frequently using the product, talking about it and integrating it in their workflows

+

familiar with product features and excited about using them to make their working lives easier

+

comfortable in using the product on an everyday basis

PDF to ABC Scoring:

BEE Insights tool:

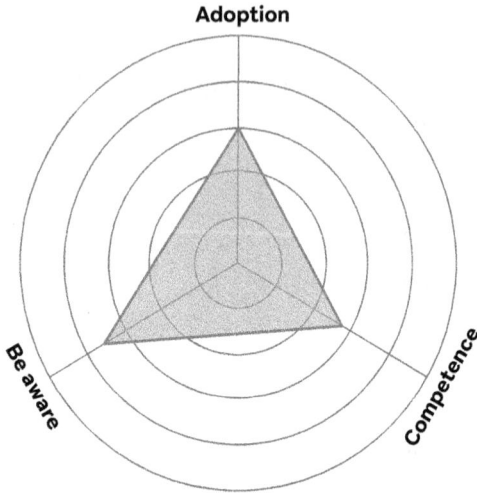

Results from an ABC Scorecard completed before adoption begins, showing an average score of 2.5 across the three categories

Knowing people's departure points for their change journeys helps you understand whether you should be focusing your time with them in the Excite phase or the Equip phase; whether people need to be brought on board with the general idea of change; or whether they just need training to adopt to the change, or both.

My current scorecard is B.

I am aware of a change happening but I'm not willing or competent yet.

Adoption

Be Aware

Competence

Your instructions for this one:

1. Transfer my questions into a suitable online tool or fill out the questionnaire available through BEE Insights.

2. Send it to everyone affected by the business change; remember to include a deadline.

3. Pull the data together.

4. Analyse the data.

5. Use this data to inform the change journey of the affected individuals.

Change freeze plan: Every business change has a time

Finding yourself a little overwhelmed by the enormous task of balancing people's calendars and commitments (as well as their emotions, thoughts and actions) while keeping your project on track (with all its milestones, budgets, and deadlines) is completely normal. It is quite a challenge, but I know you're up to it.

Because you are now starting to navigate between processes and people, you are also beginning to understand the organisation as a whole and are now best placed to position your project. As much as you're accommodating and working around other people's calendars, you're also becoming attuned to the flows and rhythms of your organisation and the dynamics of its interactions, as you've done through all the exercises in the Build phase. You know who sits at the social intersections of your company, who the go-to fixer-of-all-problems is, who secretly struggles the most and who couldn't care less.

You know all these things because you've got data and a strong gut feeling. Now, you just need to know one more thing: the timing.

Choosing the right timing, whether for beginning any business change or in the process of it, has enormous potential to create momentum and generate buy-in from people across the organisation; this will help your change project to move forward successfully. With the gravity of the change in mind, the anticipated duration and an understanding of the resources required, you'll need to decide when to get the conversation started and when to reignite it, all by working along hierarchies, grapevines and value chains. While it is simply not possible for me to tell you what *is* a good time (think: context + knowledge + co-ordination + patience), I can give you a few ideas of what *isn't*.

I like to call this bad time 'change freeze' – probably the most diplomatic synonym ever for 'Don't you dare touch this process right now'. This is intentional: business change management is about just that, being diplomatic while not forgetting to stay human and relatable. Be kind and (to a reasonable extent – don't bend over backwards) try to consider what is going on in your industry, your organisation and your project team, as well as with your change agents, social intersections, go-to's, well-being facilitators and whatever and whomever else you have identified as important in your earlier investigations.

A few tips:

- People don't like fearing the worst *(and people tend to do that in times of uncertainty)* just before Christmas when they just want to spend a few peaceful days with their loved ones.

- Changing core processes right at the end of the fiscal year might not sit well with the people in Accounts who are doing everything in their power to get the balance sheets right *(to assure the organisation's ability to carry on business)*.

- The majority of the IT team attends a five-day training session every October and won't be around to assist with the high frequency of technological breakdowns that just always seem to happen in times of change.

- Your organisation's chef, the notorious Frankie – the most popular person around and the last resort when all things fail – is away on vacation for three weeks.

- Remember: the summer holidays are not the right time to change anything but your position on the sunbed – *but I probably didn't even need to say that.*

CASE STUDY: RIVER CONSTRUCTION

For River Construction, I put together a detailed **training plan** which included bitesize training videos, training PDFs, live demonstrations and webinars for each of the products being released to the company. This training was scheduled regularly and each session followed the same patterns so that colleagues could become familiar with the offering and therefore were more likely to attend as it became part of their weekly routine.

A detailed training plan for River Construction

Title	Type of Training	Morning Session	Afternoon Session
Why you need Teams and Planner in your life	Webinar	09/02/2021 08:00	11/02/2021 15:00
Why you need OneDrive in your life	Webinar	11/02/2021 08:00	18/02/2021 15:00
Why you need Microsoft To Do in your life	Webinar	23/02/2021 08:00	25/02/2021 15:00
Live Teams and Planner demo	Webinar	10/02/2021 08:00	24/02/2021 15:00
SPO live demo	Webinar	11/02/2021 08:00	18/02/2021 15:00
Why you need Office tools in your life	Webinar	02/03/2021 08:00	04/03/2021 15:00
Why you need Lists in your life	Webinar	09/03/2021 08:00	09/03/2021 15:00

Build, Excite, Equip.

Title	Type of Training	Morning Session	Afternoon Session
Why you need Planner in your life	Webinar	16/03/2021 08:00	18/03/2021 15:00
Why you need Yammer in your life	Webinar	23/03/2021 08:00	25/03/2021 15:00
Why you need to integrate Microsoft apps into Teams	Webinar	30/03/2021 08:00	01/04/2021 15:00
Why you need Chat on Teams in your life	Webinar	06/04/2021 08:00	08/04/2021 15:00
The best of Microsoft 365	Webinar	20/04/2021 08:00	22/04/2021 15:00
How colleagues of River Construction have used Microsoft 365	Webinar	27/04/2021 08:00	29/04/2021 15:00
Why you need SharePoint Online in your life	Webinar	13/04/2021 08:00	15/04/2021 15:00
Bitesize champion training	Champion training	Every Wednesday 3pm, April–June	
Champion Forum	Q&A session	Last Thursday of Month	
Team-specific champion training	Team-specific training	Ongoing through April–June	
Team-specific training demonstrations	Team-specific training	Ongoing through April–June	
Training videos	Bitesize training	On knowledge platform	
Training PDFs	Bitesize training	On knowledge platform	

I also created a **communication plan** that targeted both the company as a whole, for widespread adoption, and the relevant individual teams and departments, as part of the targeted adoption of the content and collaboration tools.

A communication plan for River Construction

	M 11-May	T 12-May	W 13-May	T 14-May	F 15-May	M 18-May	T 19-May	W 20-May	T 21-May	F 22-May
Yammer modern digital workplace (MDW) group	To Do: Coming Soon		OneDrive: Case Study		Yammer: 'Top Tips'	To Do: Is Here		Stream: Case Study		To Do: 'Top Tips'
MDW knowledge site	Yammer: Case Study and 'Top Tips' To Do: live event Whiteboard: Coming Soon					OneDrive: Case Study and 'Top Tips' To Do: live event recording Whiteboard: training materials; live event invites				
LMS						To Do: Training videos				
The week ahead email	To Do: Coming Soon				To Do: Is Here; provide content	To Do: Is Here				Whiteboard: Coming Soon; provide content
News summary email						Yammer: Case Study and 'Top Tips'; provide content			Yammer: Case Study and 'Top Tips' article	
Regional newsletters					To Do: Coming Soon Yammer: Case Study and 'Top Tips'					Whiteboard: Coming Soon Stream: Case Study and 'Top Tips'
Intranet						MDW update: content provided		MDW: update		

I drew up a **targeted engagement plan**, researching all communication channels available to me as well as creating some that were project specific, using the M365 products that River Construction was rolling out; this enabled our communications to double up as effective demonstrations.

A targeted engagement plan for River Construction

Title	Who to	Content	When	Who Creates	Who Sends
Senior leadership team engagement email	SLT	M365 Update Buy-in for roll out Nomination of Change Agent to work with Change Team	T-25	Change Lead	Change Lead
Change agent engagement email	Change agent	M365 Update Outlining the plans for roll out Ask to further discuss the process	T-20	Change Lead	Change Lead
Understanding number of team sites	Change agent	Confirmation of desired team sites to be set up	T-18	Business Analyst	Business Analyst
Raising awareness to everyone involved	All team	What, why, when – Key message and product information	T-15	Change Lead	SLT
Social network analysis (SNA) email	All team	Link to SNA explanation of what it is and why it is important	T-12	Change Lead	SLT
Champion engagement email	Champions	You have been chosen to be champion Invite to Champion webinar Invite to Champion Yammer Group	T-10	Change Lead	SLT
ABC Scorecards	All team	Link to ABC Scorecards Explanation of what they are and why they are important	T-9	Change Lead	SLT
Invite to team-specific demonstration webinars	All team	Encourage to attend training Outline what is covered in training session	T-5	Change Lead	Change Lead
Champion and influencer recap email	Champions	Recap of what has been done so far and information of what is coming up	T-4	Change Lead	Change Agent

Title	Who to	Content	When	Who Creates	Who Sends
'It's coming' email	All team	Telling them when they will get access to the products Direction to additional training material Direction to support	T-2	Change Lead	Change Agent
'It's here' email	All team	You have access Give direction to support and training material Enjoy!	T	Change Lead	Change Agent
How is it going? Go-live follow-up email	All team	Follow up to remind all team to use the products	T+10	Change Lead	Change Agent
Email for volunteers for a case study	Champions	Ask for volunteers to speak about their experience of the products to share company wide	T+20	Change Lead	Change Lead
ABC Scorecards revisit	All team	Resend ABC Scorecard link with an explanation as to why we repeat them	T+20	Change Lead	SLT
Reinforcement email	All team	Direction to support, training materials and case studies	T+25	Change Lead	Change Agent

Another aspect I was sure to pay attention to was to consider if there was any need for **change freeze** during the project. For example, I had a situation where one of the main influencers for a particular team, who was extremely enthusiastic about getting his team on board with the tools, was on holiday for two weeks. I knew I needed him to endorse the change, and there would be a lower chance of success if I attempted to introduce the new tools to the team while he was away so this needed a change freeze.

Another example was of an occasion when the whole team would be working on-site for a few weeks with little access to their laptops or the internet. It would have been ineffective to introduce new IT products at this time. In addition, as I was starting to roll out the main products in the Spring, I had to consider the Easter weekend; this is a holiday celebrated around the world, so I had to make sure our plans avoided any go-lives around these dates.

All three of these are reasons why looking into change freeze is important to ensure you are releasing the products at a suitable time to create the most successful environment for the adoption.

A change freeze plan for River Construction

W/C		MARCH				APRIL				MAY			
	1	8	15	22	29	5	12	19	26	2	9	16	23
Team 1		Influencer OOO											
Team 2										Team On-site			
Team 3						Audit Week							
All Company							Easter			Bank Holiday			

Finally, I looked at the company, the project and the individuals involved in the change and their experiences, as part of the agreed success measures. Before I started engagement around the products, I measured individuals' **adoption success** by sending our ABC Scorecards to the individuals involved in the change, and I measured it again after I went live with the products, and then compared their results.

Before the change, Jess's assessment came back with a score of B; this meant that she was aware of the products and their benefits but did not know how to use them. By the end of the project, her assessment came back as a score of ABC, meaning she was using the products and understood how they were benefiting her. This is an example of a successful adoption. When this happened, I congratulated Jess and all others with an ABC score and reinforced the products in a closure email.

88% of people involved in the change at River Construction improved their score.

My experience with Pedro was slightly different. At the start of the project he scored neither A, B or C, meaning he had little awareness of what the products were, how they were used or how he could benefit. After the go-live, he scored an AB: he had become aware of the products and their benefits, but he still didn't really understand how to use them. Being aware of this knowledge gap meant that I could send out the training resources to Pedro and anyone else who had not yet achieved a C (for Competence) so that they could continue to learn about these once the project had closed.

Using the information obtained from individuals meant that I was able to quantify and celebrate the success of the adoption on a personal level. I then collated and analysed the data to establish how the company had adopted the products, and therefore determine whether the project had been a success.

For example, I looked at the following questions to provide more detail on the colleagues' knowledge:

- **Do you know how these products will aid your work?** 85% improved their score on this question meaning that, overall, the company understood the product benefits.

- **Do you feel comfortable using Microsoft Teams, Microsoft Planner and SharePoint Online?** 88% improved their score on this question, meaning that the vast majority of the company understood how to use the products effectively.

Adoption Success Definition table for River Construction, illustrating how you can monitor your wins to keep on track

Achieve	Description	Measure	Success Criteria for Alpha	Not Achieved
Adoption	Uptake and usage	ABC Scorecards	70% of people have an A on their ABC Scorecard	Target those without an A and provide further information on production benefits, including examples of behavioural change

Achieve	Description	Measure	Success Criteria for Alpha	Not Achieved
Product uptake	Statistics on number of downloads	In-app data: downloads	70% of people have logged on to Teams, SharePoint and Planner at least once	Liaise with their change agents (influencers and champions) for additional encouragement
Sustained product usage	Product is being used on a regular basis	In-app data: channel messages, files shared etc	70% are using the main features of the tools on a daily basis	These would be considered negative change players so will receive additional support to encourage change adoption
Be Aware	Understanding why the change is needed	ABC Scorecards	70% have a B on their ABC Scorecard	Working with the influencers to increase awareness
Behavioural change	Alpha members will understand the behavioural impact this change will make to them	Meeting attendance figures	90% of users attended a meeting where the impact matrix was explored	Repeat impact matrix meetings
Product awareness	Alpha members understand the key benefits of each product	ABC Scorecard: Do you know how these products will aid your work?	90% have increased their score for this question	These would be considered negative change players so will receive additional support to encourage change adoption
Willingness to change	Users are willing to adopt these products	ABC Scorecard: Are you excited to use Teams, Planner and SharePoint?	90% have increased their score for this question	These would be considered negative change players so will receive additional support to encourage change adoption
Competence	Knowledge, ability and experience	ABC Scorecards	50% of users have a C on their ABC Scorecard	Tailor reinforcement to areas which have been a struggle
Confidence in using the product	People are satisfied and feel able to use the products	ABC Scorecard: Do you feel comfortable using Teams, Planner and SharePoint	90% of have increased their score for this question	These would be considered a negative change player so will receive additional support time to encourage them to adopt the change

Achieve	Description	Measure	Success Criteria for Alpha	Not Achieved
Training attendance	Members have attended training	Webinar statistics	60% of users have attended at least one training session	Advertise the webinar recordings using communication channels and promotion through horizon so that they reach a wider audience
Increased collaboration	Alpha members feel that it is now easier to collaborate	Yammer polls and conversations	50% feel collaboration has improved	Outline key collaboration benefits in reinforcement phase and provide feedback loop
Increased productivity	Users feel activity has increased	Yammer polls and conversations	50% feel more productive	Outline key productivity benefits in reinforcement phase and provide feedback loop

BUILD PHASE SUMMARY

Investigate your Organisation

- ○ *Corporate Survey*
- ○ *Organisational Chart*
- ○ *Organisation Assessment*

Get to know your People

- ○ *Key Stakeholder Engagement Evaluation*
- ○ *Social Network Analysis*

Plan your Project

- ○ *Project management plan*
- ○ *Project mission statement*
- ○ *Successful Adoption Definition*
- ○ *Adoption Success Rating*
- ○ *Formulate action plans:*
  - — *Training plan*
  - — *Communication plan*
- ○ *Change freeze plan*

PART III
EXCITE

Excite

| Create | Inform | Market |

11

THE EXCITE PHASE
TIME TO ACCELERATE

As your business change finally starts taking effect, you will desperately want to see people bouncing up and down with excitement. That you will be feeling this way makes all the sense in the world: you've been investing significant time and effort into making their work routines more effective or economically more efficient by introducing new solutions. I know that of course you will be hoping that they see the benefits and appreciate your good intentions, even if it initially feels like a huge disruption, won't you?

This absence of excitement for anything that brings uncertainty and instability into your lives, as your project does, is hardwired into our brains, as we've seen. In this phase we will explore how this natural tendency can be overcome.

Well, you know what they say about good intentions and the road to hell... It's a long way from there to actual excitement for change.

What is the Excite phase?

The Excite phase is about how to engage people in the journey through creating support materials and a brand identity, informing and engaging people with these materials, and selling the change. In this phase you will launch the project.

Initiation	Design	Build	Go Live	Close

PM Activities / Deliverables / Stage Gates

Build   **E**xcite

Organisation
Define our business / culture
Understand our resources
Understand the
organisational maturity

People
Engage key stakeholders

Project
ABC Scorecards
Begin training channels
and plans
Communication strategy
Establish timelines and
recognise change freeze

People
Engage key stakeholders
Influencers and champions
Access change players

Create marketing
campaign

Inform and engage
influencers and champions

Engage people

Sell the change

Prepare the Equip phase

Stage Gates checks defined within PMO governance

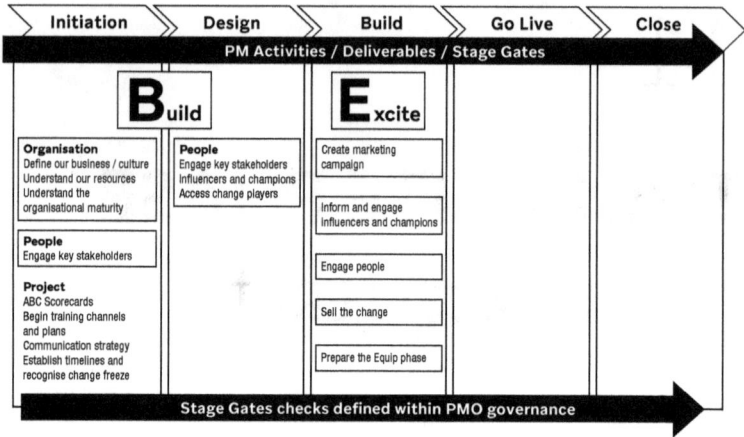

How Build and Excite can overlay your project framework

In the Excite phase you will:

- **Create** your marketing campaign

- **Inform** and engage your influencers and champions, and the people impacted by the change

- **Market** and sell the change

- Prepare for the Equip phase

The neuroscience of change (Part II)

In Chapter 7 we had a brief introduction to the neuroscience of change and explored people's natural aversion to the unfamiliar. This is the departure point for understanding the importance of an adjustment period before your business change is rolled out – that's the Excite phase I've been talking about.

So, rewind. Change induces a fear of loss and inhibits progress as it is experienced as a serious threat by the people.

I'd like to pick up where I left off with the neuroscience and explain why it matters so much to rally the troops early.

People feel scared and threatened by change of any kind, which is never a good thing and certainly not helpful in your situation. To work through feelings of loss, inhibition and threat, I've encouraged you to talk to people and listen to their thoughts and concerns, so that you can begin understanding their difficulties and formulating your action plans accordingly. Has that happened yet? If not, it should, because you need to start walking the talk. You need to lend people a hand and help them out of the fear pit. That's where neuroscience comes in again.

We're merely scratching the surface of behavioural neuroscience here, in a location somewhere near where psychology and biology intersect. Since you're probably not training to be a neuroscientist or a psychologist, we're not going to go down the rabbit hole of the exact delineation. Instead, I'd just like to focus on what I think is relevant for you as business change manager in the making: the rollercoaster of emotions that people generally experience when they are faced with change on the doorstep. That rollercoaster is commonly known as the Fear, or Change Curve, or in more scientific circles as the Kübler-Ross Change Curve®.[25] Let's take a closer look.

The origin of this is a 1969 psychological study by Dr Elisabeth Kübler-Ross on terminally ill patients who are facing their own deaths.[26] She outlines 'the five stages' (variously known as the stages of death, grief or loss), the five different emotional states experienced by these patients: denial, anger, bargaining, depression and acceptance. Since its original publication, this notion of the five stages has been widely used across a variety of sectors and modified to become what is now often understood in the business world as a four-stage sequence of emotions – denial, anger, acceptance and commitment – that can be found in everyday life and work situations when people are confronted with change.

The Change Curve

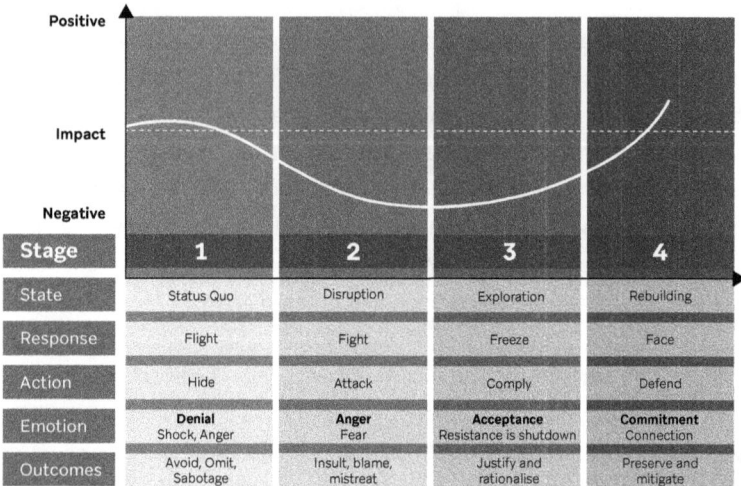

Stage	1	2	3	4
State	Status Quo	Disruption	Exploration	Rebuilding
Response	Flight	Fight	Freeze	Face
Action	Hide	Attack	Comply	Defend
Emotion	**Denial** Shock, Anger	**Anger** Fear	**Acceptance** Resistance is shutdown	**Commitment** Connection
Outcomes	Avoid, Omit, Sabotage	Insult, blame, mistreat	Justify and rationalise	Preserve and mitigate

Let's look at this four-stage model in the context of your business change project. We shall consider Stage 1 to be the starting point, the status quo; this is the dangerous place of 'this is how it's always been done' where people would comfortably remain until the end of time. The announcement of your project is going to first instigate denial, because people fear and dread change. You'll then see a fast discharge of energy, as people become anxious about the situation, frustrated about having to put up with the disruption of a complete overhaul, and angry about their lack of choice. This is Stage 2 and it will continue until you collectively hit 'empty', the point where there's no energy left to drain and the attack and blame strategies are exhausted.

From there, you'll notice that people begin eventually to come to terms with what's happening and begin exploring, with themselves and others, what their role is going to be in all of this – Stage 3. Those negotiations often become a time for people to bring up work politics and grievances, and it often becomes a period of unhelpful gossip and destructive infighting as people try to rationalise and justify their own position. These processes can become quite cumbersome and the difficult conversations can seem endless and depressingly pointless, or even unhelpful.

Eventually, and what can seem frustratingly slowly, the masses will generate enough momentum (because business does go on) to shake off their inertia and figure out the new ways of working. This can occur either because they have no choice and can't get around adoption, or because they've had great leadership in transitioning to a new status quo (which is what you're aiming for, if you were wondering). This is when they move to Stage 4.

> Why not look at the Change Curve and note down where your key stakeholders currently lie? Keep an eye on these throughout your project; make sure you update these scores and your notes frequently during the project to show their progression.

What Excitement has to do with it

Having gone through a very (very!) basic version of the Change Curve, I can finally instruct you on your two points of attack for the Excite phase.

Your first mission: Preventing people from getting stuck in denial and anger

If you give people a chance to warm up to the idea of change before you start rolling out your project, you may be able to avoid a rapid downturn on the curve and the formation of a deep, dark fear pit. It is helpful to set expectations early (as with so many things in life) and explaining what is happening and why gives everybody time to vent, complain, discuss, swear or whatever else they need to do to adjust to the uncertainty. In my experience, the path of the curve takes a much gentler drift down when people have the luxury of a period of time for personal and mental adjustment before the business change marketing campaign is launched and things get real.

Rather than simply dropping a bomb into the organisation on the day of your official business change kick-off ceremony, consider taking an exploratory approach to potential – and even hypothetical – product or process improvements; this is often usefully undertaken in collaboration with others. Strategically pick your organisation's opinion leaders and members of the Grapevine Club to talk to about your ideas and potential solutions – they'll spread the word and influence opinion faster than the running bird off Looney Tunes. People tend to take the news better when it comes from their peers rather than somewhere higher up in the hierarchy (think of yourself here); shock tends to be less damaging and deeply rooted when it can be digested in small increments.

Obviously, eventually you will have to come out with the official announcement and unveil your game plan – no question there. You'll have your project brand identity and marketing campaign in place (which I'll come to soon) and you'll be shouting about your project from the rooftops. By then, however, the whispers of change that you've strategically started will have already made it through the corridors and crept into the canteen, so now they are ready to grow into a serious roar.

> Excitement for change starts with the art of subtlety. The art of boldness (aka campaigning) comes after.

Your second mission: Preparing for people's speedy recovery from depression

As much as you want to prevent a rapid downturn of the curve in the denial and anger phases, you also need to promote a rapid upturn afterwards to ensure that you come out of the bargaining and depression phases quickly. To do that, you're going to put in place a grand campaign strategy that tells people all about the purpose of the change, the direct benefits it'll have once adopted, the awesomeness of doing it together and the resources that will be provided to quickly learn what's new.

In theory, I have now come to the part where you 'go bold' (in reality, you'll get there when you've broken the news). Grab that megaphone and start to shout from the rooftops. *Or perhaps the table tops, depending on your comfort level with heights and your organisation's health and safety regulations.* However you do it, people need to feel, see and

Tackle change depression by keeping people company throughout the process, both in person and in digital form.

hear your presence constantly once you've announced the change. While of course you can't be everywhere at the same time, you can certainly get your champions and influencers to fill in for you when you're not around. In all the places where even they can't be, make sure that people still see and recognise your project with logos, merchandise, posters and what not. Consider every human and computer touchpoint; this is the reason behind the importance of the brand identity, which we will cover in the next chapter. Now, back to driving up the Change Curve.

Another way of counteracting change depression is by lining up an abundance of digital resources (beautifully branded, of course) in a specially designed knowledge platform that anyone can access at any time, to self-solve any issue they might have. People will need to access and make use of information in their own time; creating one centralised point of reference for all learning materials will allow for highly individual learning journeys.

Therefore, here are my tip tips:

- Base your knowledge platform on a clear and simple structure. It's no use having a system in place that people need additional training to use, on top of everything else.

- Integrate a bulletproof search function into your knowledge platform. We're a search engine society and used to simple keywords giving us useful answers to complex problems.

Getting the word out: Rethinking communication

The most important lesson of this chapter is simple but something that I cannot champion enough. In the Age of Online, people have developed a weird habit of hiding behind screens all day and doing all their work and life things from right there in their study. You can actually go a whole day without speaking to anyone in person these days – it's insane what digital communication has done to us.

I can't stress enough how important it is to get out of your chair, abandon your screen for a minute and show yourself as the face of the change in as many ways as you can think of. Always remember that it's genuinely difficult for people to form a significant relationship with an online announcement and come to believe in the profound magic of transformational change. It just doesn't work like that.

Please take a minute and remember the good old days when you asked for help from an actual person rather than a search engine; when responses came in real time rather than with a 'sorry my inbox is overflowing' delay (or even worse, an automated 'I'm busy, I'll get back to you as soon as I can' message); when you used to receive one specially selected postcard in the mail rather than thirty-seven photos on a messenger app; when you used situational gestures, signals and signs rather than the thumbs-up emoji; and when your life wasn't governed by notifications and backlogs all the time.

One email after another pinging into your inbox from people you aren't allowed to ignore can feel like a four-year old impatiently and repeatedly tapping you on the shoulder with their annoyingly pointy index finger. While I admit that irritation was also a part of good old-fashioned in-person communication, I have to confess that I miss that significantly less than I do receiving postcards in the mail. However, although I casually described these constant interruptions as 'annoying' just now, researchers have found that the scale of the email demands are often experienced as 'overloading'; this can have a negative impact on the transformational leadership behaviour of managers.[27] Emails are the source of a good amount of workplace frustration, with a recent survey finding that 48% of those surveyed consider emailing to be 'the most irritating task in their day-to-day duties'.[28]

The takeaway from this chapter should be that emails can't generate excitement; quite the opposite, actually. They've become the biggest burden in the workplace over the last few years, so to cut through that and to get your change message out there, I'd like to challenge you to put your heart out there and, if it feels right, spice up the mundane communication and information culture at work with some of that spirit from the good old days. A place to start might be swapping the sterile term 'communication' with an action verb such as 'engaging', 'involving', 'interacting' or simply 'speaking'. Make the whole thing less awkward and you'll soon start to behave more like a normal person.

Your communication at this stage should be considered as a combination of officially informing people of the business change on the one hand and engaging them with exciting buy-in messaging on the other. Understanding how best to convey the former is straightforward enough and will be guided by your earlier data on people's preferred communication channels and ideal frequency; the latter requires you to tap into perception and emotion – like the marketing and sales people – and for that you need to understand *why* you are undertaking your project.

Every project has a 'Why'

Understanding the 'Why' is vital throughout your project. Take a moment to put yourself in the shoes of someone experiencing change: what sort of questions would be racing through your mind? They might include some of these:

- Why is this happening?
- Why is it happening to me?
- Why should I accept this change?

These questions are just examples. Yes, there will be many different 'why' questions, depending on both the individual and their position. For example, someone in a financial role would probably have a number of 'why' questions concerning the financial benefit to the business, whereas a person in sales may need their 'why' answered as a benefit to customers. Remember that by now you should have gained a better understanding of the culture and people in your organisation due to the work undertaken in the Build phase of the project.

Practising answering these important 'why' questions for yourself will help you prepare how best to explain the benefits of the project to an entire organisation. It is important to consider the 'why' questions for your project right from the start: don't be shy about leaning on your senior stakeholders to start answering these 'why' questions; you can feed the answers you receive into your communications throughout. Both the questions and the answers to 'why' will need to adapt and evolve to feed into the key messages, as we discuss later in the book.

Communication: The hook, four W questions and an H

Once you've defined the 'why' for your stakeholders, you'll find yourself with a list of key messages that you can use as the foundation of your communication in future. The next focus is to consider how we now fill out these messages so that they are more than just lists of key details, without over-contextualising or risking overwhelming (or overloading) the recipients.

From the start of this book, I have promised you simplicity, and that is exactly what we need from the communications. There are several tools and tricks for strong communication writing, and like everything else, I strongly recommend that you lean on subject expertise when you can, ie communication leads in the business. Just in case you do find yourself writing the communications, I have a favourite method that has served me well throughout my career and I would like to share it with you: the inverted triangle.

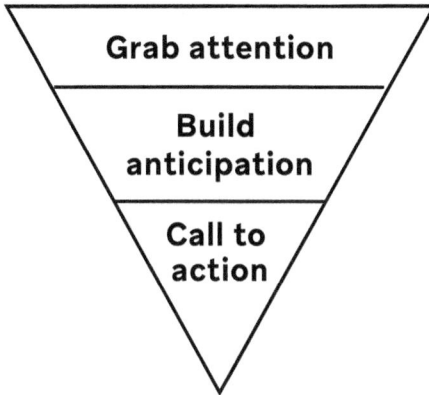

```
\           Grab attention        /
 \                               /
  \           Build             /
   \       anticipation        /
    \                         /
     \       Call to         /
      \       action        /
       \                   /
        \                 /
         \               /
          \             /
           \           /
            \         /
             \       /
              \     /
               \   /
                \ /
```

Imagine yourself skim reading an email or glancing at an advert in a magazine. You will notice that there is often a title or a prominent bit of text to catch your eye. This is the hook, or lead; it's the way to grab your attention and pique your interest, and it is the most important part of any communications.

Think about your communications. What makes them stand out to others? For those skimming the information, what can you say to make them stop and read yours? At this point you need to think about the four W questions: 'Who?', 'What?', 'Why?', 'When?', and the single H: 'How?'. Remember that the answers to 'Why?' are usually your key messages. Consider your answers to these five types of questions first and they will help you generate awesome catchy communications. Consider this example:

Who: All colleagues currently using emails

What: Emails are changing

Why: To improve productivity, collaboration, security and save time

When: 12 April

How: Automatic switchover

This becomes the basis of what you write in the leading and anticipation-building part of the communication. This is the simple part – now it's all about getting creative. Of course, you now know your culture and organisation well and have a good feeling for the type of language that is appropriate.

In our example, its internal facing only, in an open-minded and vibrant organisation:

Title: Fancy saving time with your inbox?

Hi <name>,

Guess what? We have exciting news. All colleagues are getting a shiny, brand new inbox on 12 April.

We would like to help you by increasing your productivity, saving you time and ensuring that you can collaborate even more easily with your teams. An additional bonus is that this upgrade will improve security and keep your emails safer.

By this point, you will have grabbed the readers' attention (or not). From here, they will either stop reading (having read enough to have some idea what's going on) or they will keep reading, so now is the moment to add your call to action. Put down the next steps, provide links to more information etc and ensure that you have your knowledge platform referenced (usually as a URL).

This upgrade will happen automatically overnight on 11 April, and therefore there is nothing specific for you to do other than learn more about the cool new features of the upgrade.

We have plenty of training available which we encourage colleagues to access here: <insert URL>

If you require more information, you can reach out to the team here: <insert team contacts>

Looking forward to upgrading with you.

Inbox Upgrade Team (please use a catchier name).

This example is for an email (written communication), but this format is easily transferred into other communication methods such as adverts, digital marketing etc. We shall explore that further in the next chapter, 'Create'.

And then there was data...

What comes in particularly handy at this point is the data on people's communication experiences and preferences that you've already collected and analysed in the Build phase via the Organisation Assessment, Key Stakeholder Engagement Evaluation and Social Network Analysis. You now understand all about how and when people like to receive information and where the gossip travels. Your data has told you precisely what percentage of your people find email works for them (despite me having just shred the concept of email into pieces) or whether they prefer messenger services, personal meetings or even carrier pigeons; you also know whether your people feel they hear about what's going on often enough and who sits in the epicentres of peer communication and interaction.

Remember to use a variety of different methods to suit everyone in your audience.

Use that information to keep in touch with people. Keeping in touch is a million-dollar move.

Data-to-person advances

In your data, especially your Social Network Analysis, you want to pay extra attention to those epicentres of peer communication and interaction that I mentioned earlier. These are the people that others repeatedly identified as their 'go-to's'. Those who help – the champions – and rally – the influencers – are the real weave in the social fabric and your best shot at achieving peer access to the masses. Champions and influencers can help you keep in touch with people, because they have the precious gifts of authenticity and empathy which have enabled them to gain respect and reputation among their peers. Not that you don't. It's just that they have a massive head start.

Use the data from the communication questionnaire in the Build stage to note all the communication channels available to you and their relative popularity. Rate each option for how easy it is for you to use, how easy it is for your audience to digest, and how involved the communications channel owner will be to lessen your workload. In your plans, you should consider prioritising those that score most highly.

Authenticity and empathy among their peers are two of the three key ingredients to trust, and you should be smart and leverage that. When you complement their skills with your rigorous logic (communication and training plans loading...), you create a business change environment with a solid foundation of trust.

Your strategy with the champions and influencers is to seek and cultivate relationships. This is even more important than with others in the organisation because these will be considered your change agents, as I'll refer to them from now on (although it does sound a little more dangerous and MI5 than intended). These are the people who can seriously help you drive the change. If those identified as change agents agree to be on your unofficial team (remember that not everyone you've identified will want to take an active part in your project), plan in a good amount of time to build connections and establish trust.

Champions and influencers are your million-dollar recruits.

Beyond an email

Before I leave you to muster your courage for in-person engagement, I thought I'd share a few ideas on how to lure people away from their screens.

Ever heard of the Swedish concept of *fika*? It's the ritual of sharing a cup of coffee (and perhaps a small bite of cake) with others at work, a moment to pause and engage socially, to talk about anything but work for fifteen minutes. Think of it not just as a ritual but as a state of mind that one cannot achieve by sitting alone at your desk. A similar idea is the Dutch *borreltje*. It's an informal or impromptu get-together at the end of the day where work colleagues grab a drink and some snacks and spend some time in relaxed conversation, to catch up and connect. It's a pretty low-key affair, but might prove to be the necessary sweetener for your champions and influencers and gives you a chance to get to know them a little better.

If there's a strong social culture at your organisation and you feel like connecting with the business change over a pint, this might make this transition process a lot smoother, so allocate a budget for the champions and influencers to take their crews out and invest in their peer social status. It's about creating a sense of companionship which might just be what people need in tough times. Although it sounds insane, making time to *not* talk about your business change project might really help your business change project. Introducing initiatives such as *fika* breaks or *borreltje* might just get you some added goodwill points among the people – but make sure to get this approved on all levels first.

If all else fails, perhaps start a game of change-themed 'pay it forward' in your organisation. The idea is to surprise someone with a small act of kindness – a note with a compliment on great work left on the desk, a motivational GIF sent during an afternoon low, a cool office mug to keep up the good spirit – and have the recipient extend the favour to someone else. Once gratitude enters the equation, it's often quite hard to feel annoyed or angry.

Get creative. As creative as your organisation allows and needs you to be.

Summary

The Excite phase is about bringing people on board and winning them over to the change agenda; it also includes the launch of the project. Over the coming chapters, we will explore the three components of the Excite phase:

- **Create:** Develop a brand identity and its key messaging, including a 'What's in it for me?' analysis.

- **Inform:** Engage with your influencers and champions to spread the word.

- **Market:** Sell the change with marketing events and communications.

It's critical throughout the Excite phase to connect with your people in person, and to support them as they work through the four-stage emotional journey of the Change Curve. Leverage your change agents in this process: the personal relationships that they have throughout the organisation are among your most powerful tools in the Excite phase.

12

CREATE

LET THERE BE MARKETING

I am super keen on strategic marketing in the context of business change projects for one simple reason: it works. More often than not, project managers forget to make themselves adequately heard, and the result is that they then fail to take people along with them for the change journey. Having plans, roadmaps and all is great (necessary even – Greetings from the Build phase...), but if nobody is mentally prepared and ready to follow them, then we all know where a project is headed. Especially one as profoundly disruptive as a business change project.

This chapter is about stepping up your game, making the transition from considering communication as an interpersonal exchange between individuals, to instead seeing it as a strategic marketing tool that sells your project to the whole organisation. I'm well aware that this might be completely new territory for you, but I'll be with you every step of the way. We're about to tackle that Change Curve head on. Remember your two missions? The two points of attack needed to shape the curve in your favour?

1. Plant the seeds of change early, so that people can warm up to the idea and the resulting period of uncertainty and disruption. I gently *(but firmly)* refer you back to the previous chapter where we discussed taking the leap into real world conversations and personal

interactions. The trick here is to take the initiative, to be involved from Day One, and *(to some degree)* let people come to believe that it was their idea to change things up in the first place. Organic works better, be it on farmers' markets or in times of change. The world has come to know that.

2. Be perfectly prepared and have a presence everywhere, all of the time. As well as your little change agent fairies, your magic potion for achieving that miracle is going to be your project marketing.

Let's cut this reality check short and move on to how to create a successful (simple but blissful) marketing strategy. To do this I'll have to make a quick detour into the land of psychology – you'll understand why in about a minute.

Understanding psychology in marketing

Have you ever been in a situation where a friend told you about XYZ over a drink on a Wednesday night and by Thursday afternoon, you're suddenly seeing and hearing about XYZ everywhere? You might find yourself inventing conspiracy theories to explain why on earth XYZ seems to be following you around all day. That, dear friend, is called the frequency illusion, or the Baader-Meinhof Phenomenon (if you want to sound fancy at your next meeting), and it is a cognitive bias that our minds create once we've been made aware of something which means that we suddenly start seeing it everywhere. This is because of two processes within the human brain, selective attention (so new stuff stays fresh in our minds and we subconsciously pay more attention to it) and confirmation bias (we subconsciously look for evidence to support what we already know or believe: that the new thing is suddenly everywhere). In combination, the two cause us to perceive the new thing more consciously and therefore inevitably we notice it more frequently, as soon as we've learned about it. We can make use of this psychological trickery in our marketing campaign: once we have made people aware of your project, we want them to notice it everywhere. The illusion of your project as being extremely popular is perfect.[29] You must recognise that creepy feeling that you are somehow being watched or influenced without your knowledge? Marketers have been using this for decades.

Rolling out a strategic marketing campaign, no matter how small, is your way of being everywhere (in a digital format) all of the time. It is your tool to reinforce the idea that your project is currently the hottest topic in your organisation, so that your project stands out to them despite the weight of work that lands on their desks every day. You need to be noticed, and every second a brain notices your project is a win, because you're competing with a ton of stimuli out there. You therefore need to make it good – a cheesy WordArt creation won't win the competition for people's attention... not in a million years. So far, so good. I've got the individual brain level covered, but do you remember the importance of considering the collective level?

There's another psychological phenomenon that works beautifully in conjunction with the frequency illusion and that is called 'social proof'. It's about people following other people's lead when they don't know what to think or how to act in uncertain situations.[30] You, me, your neighbours, your friends and colleagues, we all do it: we look to others for guidance on what to think and do. We even imitate their thoughts and behaviour, due to inherent desire to fit in and conform. Understanding that is key to seizing your opportunity to influence some useful herd behaviour – because social proofing can be quite the effective persuasion method. This is why it is imperative that you perform a Social Network Analysis, find the change agents and involve them early. Building sound relationships with them and training them carefully will enable them to help you roll out that change, utilising the power of social proof.

To sum up, with a project marketing campaign, you want people to notice you, decide you're a hot topic and then also convince their peers. Remember that rather than any of the definitions. It gets a little more practical from now on.

Creating an appealing project brand identity

Your project absolutely needs to be defined by a strong brand image, a look that is easily spotted and recognised in the hustle of a busy workday, something that you can put out there for people to notice. While I usually strive to bust jargon, I'll stick to the marketing term here because it's clean and straightforward: your project needs a brand identity. This can then be used as a visual aid when playing with people's attention, perceptions and biases, to exploit the phenomena and effects I described above.

For those hearing of 'brand' and 'identity' in the context of the workplace for the first time, they're integral elements of strategic marketing. Brand is defined by a subject expert as follows: your brand is 'a definition of an emotional relationship between customers and the business'.[31] In your context, that would be people's gut feeling about your project. Brand is a powerful connection between people and the project, and with your brand you're making a 'promise' to the people, so that they can believe in you.

Jeff Bezos (the Amazon guy) famously described your brand as 'what other people say about you when you're not in the room'.[32]

More important is your brand identity (it gets a little less conceptual and a little more tangible now). Returning to our subject expert, 'Brand identity is what you can see. It fuels recognition, amplifies differentiation and makes big ideas and meaning accessible.'[33] It is the visual appearance of your brand, and how you remind the people of the promise and value you offer.

When creating a brand identity for your project, you need to decide what the underlying design for every presentation slide and every printed poster related to your business change will be. Do yourself a favour and don't go searching online for this stuff too much. Branding is an art rather than a science and the delineation between brand, brand identity and related concepts is blurry and extremely confusing. The point here is to create an appealing visual design for your project that you can use continuously and consistently on all materials (digital and nondigital) that concern your project, not to become the next big branding specialist.

To find out whether you can take on the temporary role of brand identity designer yourself, I've prepared a quick exercise that helps with the evaluation of design capabilities in your project team and organisation. If you've already decided whether or not you'll create the design yourself, you might find the Project Brand Identity Checklist useful. The list is a compilation of the skills that you need to further develop your marketing materials. One thing that I would certainly recommend is preparing a Campaign Kit Checklist for when you start sharing the news and meeting people in person to discuss and drive the change.

Creating convincing video messages

The creation phase isn't over yet. You're just warming up. Once the project brand identity is confirmed, your first act of producing *actual* marketing content is creating a small series of short videos on the new product or process, outlining what benefits people can expect from them. To keep it simple (I like to do that...), I call these the 'What's in it for me?' (WIIFM) videos. Take a moment here to go back to your 'Why' answers to ensure that you're capturing the WIIFM benefits, because these videos need to inform the individual about what they will get out of adopting the business change.

Such videos usually start with quick visuals presenting your organisation logo and project brand (including your slogan, icon and whatever else you came up with), and then immediately move to deliver the most important message: answering WIIFM. Whether or not you believe that our attention spans – and those of goldfish – are short and shrinking (Hey, I'm just the messenger. Take it up with BBC News, if you don't agree),[34] I just know that you need to get your message over quickly. Think of a WIIFM video as a news story, because even if someone has heard rumours in the hallways, this might be their first official touchpoint with your project and that's huge news. News stories are usually structured so that the most important information comes first, then other crucial details and finally any extra elements that the reporter wants to share. This strategy of 'front-loading' works, so stick to it. Journalists do.

When you are considering whether you have the skills to design both the project identity and the WIIFM videos, I need you to be honest. Can you pull off the creation of a project brand identity and the production of video messages yourself? Let me tell you, if you have even the smallest sliver of doubt, get help from the experts – your marketing department is a good start. If you start sending out poorly designed announcements and materials, and videos that look like relicts from the good old days of Myspace, I guarantee you're in for a major belly flop. A terrible first visual impression kills all change spirit and you'll be hearing about your ridiculous design attempt until the day you retire. I therefore strongly advise you to have a look at my WIIFM Video Checklist (see Chapter 13) to get an idea of what needs to be included in the final product.

Creating a bespoke knowledge platform

After a small excursion into the realm of marketing and sales, we're getting back on to familiar terrain. You need to get to work immediately and start creating a single reference point to contain all learning related to the new product or process. Your learning centre, resource base – call it whatever you want (I'll refer to it as your 'knowledge platform' from now on) – is going to be a collection of resources that people should be able to access anywhere, anytime, and as many times as they want on their device of choice. It will be somewhere for people to go and look at tutorials and manuals if they can't figure out how to navigate the new system.

This knowledge platform is going to be your main tool in the Equip phase and it is of immense importance that you take its development seriously, because whether your project flourishes or fails will depend on it. The better you make it, the more user-friendly the navigation, the more accurate the search function, the more people will be able to help themselves along their individual learning journeys, leaving you free to focus on the overall project progress. If you want to keep your time free to maintain a prominent visual presence and speak to people in person, to ensure buy-in on all levels (and all of that is exactly what you're going to need even if you don't know it yet), you'd better get your best person to write the code for this platform. Have them look at our Knowledge Platform Checklist too (see Chapter 13).

Here are just a few considerations before you go off and create the best platform ever. Firstly, recycle or reuse. Maybe there is already an existing system in place that you could use? If not, you can consider tapping into existing online communication tools such as Yammer or the company intranet. Either way, be sure to check with the relevant teams (including Comms, L&D and IT) as they are most likely to know.

If you find yourself without an existing resource, now is the time to get to work. Treat this like a website project. Get someone to dig into UX design and map out user journeys, start to end (one day, hopefully...), so that navigation is easy and intuitive for everyone in your organisation. Make it clean and contemporary; put effort into setting the interface apart from Windows 95 – none of us like going back to the days of garage-level design.

If you're feeling really fancy and have got the resources, think of modifying your platform for different divisions, departments or teams. People may need to learn about different aspects of the product and they speak different professional languages – think of Charlie in Accounts and Kim in Marketing who are always on slightly different pages in the same conversation. While this is obviously a question of time and money, it may be worth considering spending part of your budget on this, to shield people from information overload that could result in confusion and anger, setting back the progress of your project. A little streamlining never hurts.

Summary

To sell your change project, you're going to need a strategic marketing campaign. It's not as hard as it sounds. The key components are a strong project brand identity, convincing and compelling video messaging and a killer knowledge platform. In the next chapter I'll walk you through how to create these assets.

13

EXERCISES: CREATE

OUR CREATE TOOLS

The Excite phase is all about marketing, and for that, you'll need to create some marketing assets. First, it's a good idea to evaluate your own capabilities in design – can you do this yourself, or would it be better to engage an expert? Next, you'll need to create a visual identify for the project, a campaign kit, a WIIFM video and most important of all, the project's knowledge platform.

Evaluation of Design Capabilities

It's critical to create an appealing project visual identity, not because you want to win a design award in the Newcomer Category, but because you and your project team don't want to look like a bunch of clowns. Trying to excite people for business change with a poorly designed visual identity can seriously harm your reputation and completely undermine your project's mission and objectives. People may well forget what on earth your project is about if they're busy laughing at your WordArt creation behind your backs. Imagine how much this would hurt, not just you (you are Head of Everything these days and need to have a thick skin) but also your team members, if people endlessly made fun of your work. You have a responsibility towards your team and so make sure that you come up with a solid (we're not looking for awe-inspiring, 'solid' will do…) project visual identity that the entire team can be rightly proud of. Consider this task a way of uniting your team and the entire organisation behind a project that is up to speed with today's style and language.

To understand whether you've got what it takes to whip up a project visual identity (and all things 'design' after), take a minute to complete my flowchart exercise. Be honest with yourself in the process and, if you've got anyone on your team who you think might have the necessary skills, let them do it too.

One small heads-up: some organisations will not respond well to inventive project brand identities. Whether there are regulations in place that forbid creative play with branding or the official decision-makers are party poopers, there are situations in which I do not recommend pushing the boundaries. There's a good chance you'll already be fighting an uphill battle with your anticipated business change so making unnecessary enemies before the real hassle has even started is unwise.

If your organisation is one of those that just won't have it, you're going to have to find other ways to be memorable to your people. One option could be to unofficially take on elements of 'brand' yourself, to become more visible than ever and make sure that everyone in the organisation knows your name, your mission and how to reach you. You're going to have to get the message out somehow, and both a project visual identity and a personal outreach strategy can create the emotional bonds you so urgently need to generate buy-in.

Project Visual Identity Checklist

Your project's visual identity is the character you give the whole endeavour; it's the visual that will tell the story of your business change. Ideally, it will help people remember you and your mission, and even evoke a few emotions like connection, purpose and safety that can help build trust and establish a personal relationship to the change.

Do you know why a logo should be created as a PNG file rather than a JPEG file?

YES So far, so good

NO Fair enough

Have you ever heard of the Golden Ratio?

Can you justify a budget to hire a designer?

YES So far, so good

NO Fair enough

Comic Sans?

YES So far, so good

NO Fair enough

Is there someone on the marketing team who can help?

Go and get a professional

NO Fair enough

Do you or team members have a best buddy or partner who can help?

NO Fair enough

Are you willing to go the extra mile and learn about design as you develop your own?

YES So far, so good

NO Fair enough

Please get professional help.

Give this project to your marketing team, a creative sibling or cousin, or even a design student. It is well worth those extra few days to have someone else create something that at least looks like its from this century.

YES So far, so good

NO Fair enough

Do you have 2+ weeks to brainstorm, ideate and iterate your creation?

YES So far, so good

Do you have 2+ weeks to have your brand developed in a semi-professional arrangement?

It's time to roll up your sleeves and figure this out with your team. Get those with even an iota of experience onto the task and start working through your checklist. Do the best you can, but don't lose sleep over an imperfect design. Run it by your marketing team for general feedback and it'll be ok!

NO Fair enough

YES So far, so good

NO Fair enough

Get your chocolates ready, put your game face on and butter up the marketing department to get them to put it into their resource plans.

Can you spare 3 days?

YES So far, so good

You're in for a sweet excursion into the Land of Design, where you can play with colours and slogans, iterate your logo and integrate everything with your organisation's brand identity. The trick here is collaboration: learning how to do it and asking for help when needed. Perhaps someone in marketing has a minute to go through your ideas? Maybe someone in your team is a secret design enthusiast? Make use of expertise and enthusiasm wherever you can find it.

YES It's go time!

Activate all your resources, grab your most design-savvy team members and get to work! 3 days is not a whole lot, but you can certainly decide on a simple but effective logo (colours matched with your organisation's brand identity), a clever slogan and get a decent photo of your team.

NO It's obvious

Designing a fancy project brand identity is not a priority right now. You need to path out your project and get this show on the road. I recommend whipping up a simple design, perhaps a logo and a slogan in your company colours, and go from there.

Work through the decision tree to help determine your resources and requirements

To create the visual identity that you'll need to market your project, there are a few basics that must be considered. A professional designer would have a million things to say about the simplicity of this approach, but I'm convinced that you need practical guidance on how to dress your brand in an identity that comes across as prepared and ready. Consider the following:

- Find a project name. *Make it sound like a smash hit.*

- Get creative and pull some mood boards together that will help you decide on a direction for the imagery. Perhaps it's a contemporary style you're after, or maybe you're looking for something more classic and traditional? Maybe your company will embrace a cartoon style?

- Create a logo. This can be as simple as an icon.

- Write a slogan. *Please don't make it sound like your grandmother or Winston Churchill...*

- Select primary and secondary colours that go with your organisation's brand colours.

- Choose a font. This is likely to be your organisation brand's font.

Free user-friendly online design tools:

www.adobe.com/express
www.canva.com
www.look.com

It's important to understand the format and sizing needs of your logo or any imagery you need to create or you will end up with a pixelated, unusable image. Remember that a PNG has a transparent background, while a JPEG background is solid.

What you want to arrive at is something like this:

Example of a strong visual identity for the change project at River Construction

Now I've covered the basics, I have a small favour to ask: please don't get overconfident in your first branding endeavour or you'll lose track. Aesthetics can be a highly individual and subjective matter; while you might think that your creation looks amazing and would convince even NASA to switch, others may feel otherwise. Hold a short workshop, run a few ideas past one another and seek feedback from Kim and her colleagues in Marketing – they're probably already experts at this (and they probably won't want to market your silly WordArt 'design'). However you need to do it, just ensure you don't end up embarrassing your entire project team with something hideous like this:

Example of a poor design for the project's visual identity

If people really hate your project's visual identity, they're less likely to understand it, and they're less likely to want to be onboarded, leading to a good chance they'll end up resisting your overall change project.

The world of aesthetics can be as unforgiving as the wind in Cornwall.

Campaign Kit Checklist

At this stage in your project, your focus is on trying to catch people's attention with the right design and language and making the rounds to be present everywhere and all the time; in many ways, you're moving into territory similar to that of a political campaign before Election Day. You want people's buy-in just as much as politicians want people's votes. Isn't that right?

To come across as just as eager, prepared and keen as a politician on a campaign trail, I suggest you create a quick campaign kit. This enables you to do two things: to present a robust and consistent image everywhere you go, and to follow up on these meetings with the kind of professionalism people expect from someone who is about to revolutionise their decade-old working practices. You therefore need to prepare the following:

- A clean Microsoft PowerPoint template for presentations

- A designated contact email address for thoughts, questions and complaints related to your project, so you don't miss important messages in the mess of your own inbox

- A project-branded email signature for internal communication that can be used by you, your team, your change agents, the CEO and anyone else who wants to show their support

- A nice photo of you and the project team, in case you need to introduce yourself or Marketing wants to publish an internal blog post

- A social media hashtag if you are planning a lot of events and exciting stuff that people might enjoy. This will help generate 'noise' across the social media platforms

- A printed banner for bigger gatherings, and/or posters for the lobby or cafeteria, that will repeatedly expose people to your project brand identity and help imprint it in their minds

Whatever you do, try to be a little original here. Try to use a little creative freedom in preparing your organisation's public appearance. With that, you should be all set and ready to go.

CASE STUDY: RIVER CONSTRUCTION

Wireframe example of the digital visuals from the project at River Construction

Wireframe example of a clear project presentation slide from River Construction

Wireframe example of a strong banner design from River Construction

'What's In It for Me' (WIIFM) Video Checklist

When getting ready to produce the short video messages, you must understand this: these little clips will be the first appearance of your project before your people; as they say, there is no second chance for a first impression, so make it count. I realise that you're also just beginning your content creation learning journey, but this is not the time for trial and error. This is the time to go big or go home.

To make these video messages look as slick as possible, make sure to check all boxes on the following list:

- Front-load your message, as discussed earlier.

- Be careful not to overload your videos – there's only so much you can say in a minute and a half.

- Make sure you stick to your project brand identity, with consistent brand colours, fonts etc.

- Keep it clean and simple, without it looking sterile or uninspiring.

- Use a dark font on a light background for all text. This will stand out and is also more accessible.

- Choose images of a similar style that work with your choice of colours.

- Pick someone with a clear and pleasant voice to narrate the project story.

- End on a motivational note.

I strongly recommend that you stay away from the special effects that remind people of terrible Microsoft PowerPoint animations; they look incredibly cheap and will cause the kind of reactions behind your back that you want to avoid at all costs.

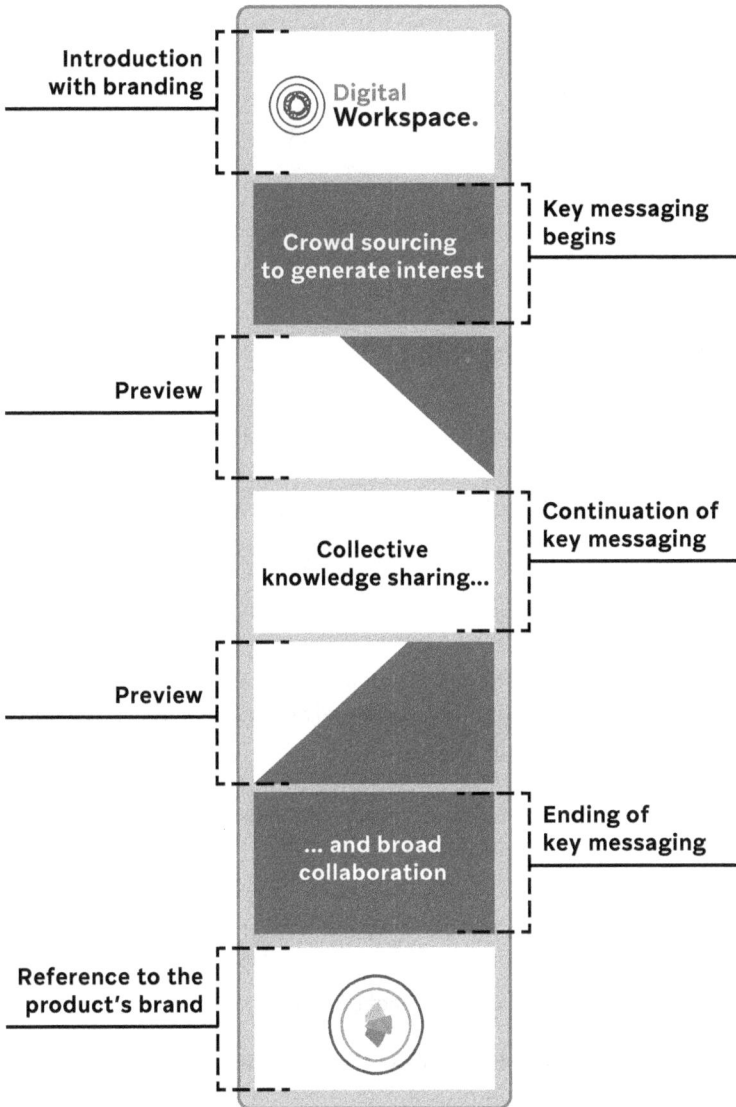

Introduction with branding

Digital
Workspace.

Key messaging begins

Crowd sourcing to generate interest

Preview

Continuation of key messaging

Collective knowledge sharing...

Preview

Ending of key messaging

... and broad collaboration

Reference to the product's brand

A storyboard (including key messages and project benefits) for a WIIFM impact video

Build, Excite, Equip.

Check out some WIIFM video examples here:

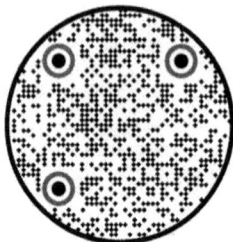

Key Message Checklist

When ensuring you have your key messages in place, there are a few things I'd encourage you to go through as part of this exercise. First, we need to think through the 'Whys' and you should do this in relation to three types of people:

- What do you consider to be the 'Whys'?

- What do your target groups consider to be the 'Whys'? For example, what would Finance consider a benefit? How would this compare to how Marketing might respond?

- Finally, consider the 'Whys' for some of the internal shared services teams such as HR or Comms.

Now get a spreadsheet or table ready, and answer the following questions:

- What are the listed project benefits?

- Why should I be bothered about these benefits?

- What are the individual benefits to each group?

- What objections would each group give? For example, Occupational Health is currently experiencing extreme growth, so may not consider time saving to be a realistic project benefit for their department right now.

Once you have these outlined your answers for each of these groups, you can then ensure these messages go into the right format, and you can tweak the language to mitigate and address any concerns you anticipate from particular departments.

Knowledge Platform Checklist

As I've said before, you should recruit your best candidate to undertake this task and be sure to give them enough time to create an exceptional library for your business change information and resources. Every bug in the system that causes someone to exit the platform early and move on with their day without gaining that extra bit of knowledge or understanding is a loss. This may sound harsh, but it is a loss that is on you, and at some point in the transition process there will have to be compensation paid for that loss. It's better to avoid losses in the first place and to have a decent knowledge platform.

You need to build this resource hosting site as if for an external client who has exceptionally high standards and won't tolerate any faults. Imagine that your ultimate KPIs are based on bounce rate, average session duration and conversions (aka business change believers), but always remember that this is for people to train themselves so keep ease of use and accessibility at the fore. Now is the time to put on your web-developer hat and start building, remembering always the following key points:

- Make the search function your biggest priority.

- Create a logical learning journey with a sequential setup. Consider how much you can tailor that journey to individual departments and teams.

- Assure availability on all common devices (use links for accessibility).

- Give people options for how to access the information: video, audio and text, as your budget allows.

- Integrate your project brand identity whenever possible.

- Consider a support chatbot or a clearly visible help button.

> Does your organisation already have a knowledge platform that you could/should use? If so, who owns it? Speak to them about whether you can use it, how and what support they can provide.

CASE STUDY: RIVER CONSTRUCTION

River Construction had an existing SharePoint Online site for their IT projects, so I was able to use this. I took a little time to improve the look and feel of the site, being sensitive to the existing information so as not to upset the current author of the site or undermine their hard work.

The first step was to create a project identity and logo for each part of the project that was included in the product awareness training. This was done to be consistent with the project brand identity and was therefore a way of ensuring that, subliminally, those individual components would still be understood in association with the overall project.

Thankfully, most colleagues were already experienced intranet users, with this as their default browser, so I created a 'teaser' banner for the home page, to catch their attention, pique their curiosity and entice them enough to want to click through to learn more.

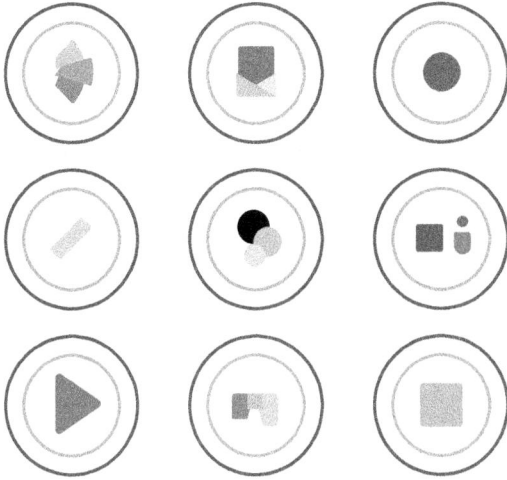

*Examples of how the logos for the various components can be
made consistent with your overall project visual identity*

Wireframe example of a 'coming soon' banner

This lovely looking banner – *yup, you've guessed it* – redirected readers straight to our SharePoint Online site. The site contained all the information they needed at each stage of the change process: this started off with basic overview information and expanded from there.

Build, Excite, Equip.

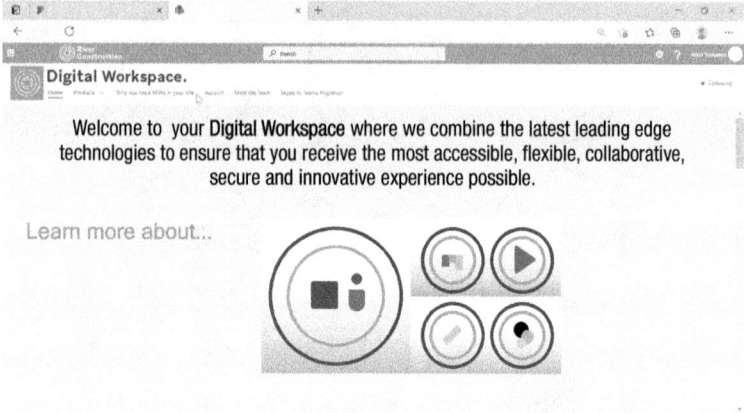

Landing page on the River Construction SharePoint Online site, with clear and easy-to-follow information and consistent branding

This URL was repeated in all communication relating to the project, with a reminder to make a habit of visiting the SharePoint Online site frequently. I even ensured that the SharePoint Online URL was a default tab on the Teams sites when it was created – that's forced marketing if ever I saw it.

14

INFORM

GENEROUSLY, BUT
STRATEGICALLY

I've talked a lot about relationships so far. I've examined how there are official outlines and unofficial tangles of relationships within an organisation (and you need to know about both) and explored how an organisation exists in the interactions and relationships of its people. We also discussed how people cannot form relationships if they don't have access to emails; if they did, that would be weird, probably unhealthy and certainly against everything we're trying to get across here.

I have no doubts that a large part of Excite – the time in which you Create and Market your project to the whole organisation – needs to be about personal engagement and real human encounters. The Inform stage of this phase is about finding the best ways to communicate with people, especially how to deploy your change agents, the champions and influencers.

When you meet somebody facing change, there can be such sincerity and vulnerability if someone is struggling, and pure delight and encouragement in someone who sees progress in change. You need to seize the opportunity to take them both by the hand and cross the finishing line together. The encounters you have and the relationships you build on this journey will be challenging and nerve-racking, but they will be equally rewarding and transformational, probably to an extent that you cannot begin to imagine.

It all leads back to neuroscience again, to pleasure chemicals and instincts, and the fact that humans are social creatures who seek connection with each other. Good relationships grow on a foundation of trust, and trust, as I've been reminded many times, is an interplay of logic, authenticity and empathy.[35]

Business change can be as touching as watching your best buddy get married.

By this stage, I expect you to be done developing your logic and I hope that personal encounters will help you gain confidence to show your authentic self. Let's therefore focus on empathy for just a second, because it is going to be your strongest lever moving forward with your project. Empathy describes your ability to identify with and understand the wants, needs and viewpoints of those around you – putting yourself in another's shoes or seeing the world through someone else's eyes, if you will.

Empathy matters so much because you're making the project public and getting ready for a complete overhaul; because it is your key to understanding where someone is on their change journey; because only then can you figure out how to help them overcome their individual difficulties and successfully adopt the change. Empathy needs to be at the heart if your project is to succeed. To bring your empathy into play, you're going to have to meet people in the flesh. There's no way around it, even if you're only just learning how to become a people person.

Communicate to inform

I know it sounds exciting and terrifying in equal measure to finally face people and share your news. To stand in front of them and tell them why they should care about, and even believe in, your project is to make yourself vulnerable and expose your weaknesses; to initiate, witness and experience emotional confrontation can shock you with your power over others; to listen to criticism so harsh you'll wish you'd never started can be soul-destroying. Some of your relationships at work are about to set off on the wrong foot and some are going to be shaken deeply, while others are just about to flourish and become a source of constructive input and collaboration. For all the fears, this is also a time bristling with excitement and potential.

You're extremely lucky if people are already supportive of your business change and able to see the project's benefits and value. If that's the case, your organisation is probably working with products and processes from around the time of the Big Bang so what you're about to introduce can only be an upgrade. If you're in a more difficult position – perhaps facing

The golden rule is never to think that you can anticipate what's coming.

disquiet and nervousness generated by an economically tough time for the business (see the Corporate Survey data), or an organisation with a particularly diverse demographic or different levels of confidence with technology (see Organisation Assessment data) – you've got a much bigger job ahead of you, and you need to begin to ascend the mountain that is building trust.

In this case, your communications need to do far more than just inform or excite. You need to speak to the masses and yet still connect to them on a deeply individual interpersonal level. The Excite phase, with all its official announcements and introductions, is the greatest opportunity to broadly demonstrate the logic in your reasoning, authenticity in your interactions and empathy in your relationships – the importance of which should be abundantly clear by now. Politicians are doing the exact same thing when campaigning, as they connect with people (personally, or so it seems) to secure their votes. You're going to connect with people to earn their buy-in, and – *attention, please* – gain their assent to walk alongside and keep them company on their journey along the Change Curve. Your only opportunity to influence the course of the curve is if people trust you enough to let you lead them through denial and anger, out of bargaining and depression and into a state of acceptance.

At this stage, you need to focus on integrating the principles of trust with the Change Curve, formulating a project marketing approach and communicating judiciously; you will have to leverage personal connection for all of these, using the data collected during the Build phase. But that's the nature of change, and let's not forget that you've got help.

Inform through the change agents

In the context of trust building and the Change Curve, I've mentioned the importance of your network of champions and influencers, your change agents. They are respected and valued by their peers like no one else in the organisation. When times are tough, these guys are your reinforced safety net; they are your million-dollar recruits, as I've put it before.

In this chapter, I am reminding you of the importance of trust and of the presence of your crew of supporters because you're reaching a point where the meetings, questions and transitions are about to begin, if they haven't begun already. With your project announcement or kick-off ceremony, you're taking a dive down the line of the Change Curve. You've got the digital bases covered – project brand, video messages and knowledge platform – so now you need to underpin any gaps or weak points with valuable and reliable people who can help buffer the fall.

From here on, you need to keep your change agents incredibly close; make sure to have them physically and mentally present as you make the rounds to get people acquainted with your project. Plan your meetings, town halls, workshops and whatever else in a way that enables the change agents of the respective divisions, departments and teams to be there with you. Once the formal part of any gathering is over, they are the ones who will take the change story back to the offices and break rooms and help people make sense of and navigate the business change. People naturally turn to their champions and influencers anyway, whether you planned for it or not. Use them.

Working so closely with your change agents can pose challenges, particularly if you find some of them harder to like or work with than others (although you really shouldn't allow yourself the luxury of disliking someone who is loved by the masses – that way failure lies). Despite this, you and your project team must cultivate close relationships with the change agents, consider their schedules in your plans, prioritise their product or process training, invite and consider their input and carve out time to meet and strategise with them, even if that means you have to bend over backwards or arrive an hour early. It is through them that you get through to people. You'd be a fool to ignore that.

Strategising with the change agents

While you're busy bringing business change to the masses, your change agents are going to be busy on an individual level, helping anybody who is struggling. Sharing work like this lets you follow a highly sustainable strategy: keeping an eye on the collective climate while supporting the individual journey to a new status quo. It goes without saying that you should express your gratitude for their efforts and commitment as often and as genuinely as you can. You should also try to learn their names: it's the least you can do when they're doing half your work.

The kind of strategising I have in mind for you and your change agents relies heavily on the close collaboration. You need to hear about their experiences with people's struggles and make time to think through the best way to approach these struggles together. It can be hard to ensure that every person affected by the business change gets their fair share of support, while also making sure that a few individuals don't monopolise the change agents' time – or your own.

Alex from PR might be in the denial phase, having missed all the rumours while on sabbatical; he's now feeling robbed of a smooth re-entry into the workplace after picking avocados on a farm in Australia for six months. Ahmad from Customer Service might generally be against anything new, constantly emphasising the benefit in 'how it's always been done'. Kim from Marketing might have already understood the reality of the situation but is just mad about not having been included in the brand identity fun. Nicky from IT might be completely fine with everything going on, pleased to have a job at all after a difficult period of unemployment, but is struggling to stay out of the crossfire between polarised colleagues. Finally, of course there's Billie, Billie from Operations, who probably deserves an award for having watched all the tutorial videos overnight, and is now talking with his colleagues about nothing but the new features and possibilities. *You know you can always rely on good old Billie from Operations.*

Billie is a perfect example of why it is so important to provide people with a well-organised and easy-to-navigate knowledge platform where they can hold themselves responsible and accountable for their own learning progress – if they've come that far on their change journey. To get people to that point, you need to hold meetings, provide trainings and engage in conversations to establish what is happening, why it's

> *A business change project is, indeed, a heap of interlacing stories. Envy, competition, circumstances... It gets as personal and messy as that.*

happening, who is affected, where everyone needs to be skill-wise and by when, and how they'll get there. Somewhere along the way, it'll get through to them all that the business change is inevitable, binding for everyone and ultimately for their benefit.

To understand how you and your change agents should prioritise your time between people, you'll need to perform another analysis, one that is not about people in general and their roles within the organisation, but one that is about individuals and their current stance in this particular project.

Determining the change players

Clearly it's totally impossible for you to create a personal Change Curve for every single person affected by, or involved in, the business change. Instead, you're going to take a shortcut and map people onto a spectrum that captures their general mood and attitude towards your project.

Perhaps you're thinking: Why did I even bother explaining the Change Curve to you if that's now what we're using? The reason is because it's important to understand the psychological stages that people go through when accepting change, because they will determine their emotions which, in turn, affects their behaviour. If you've got a hard nut to crack, someone who just won't do what you ask, you can always look more closely and trace their progress on the Change Curve to try and understand their resistance and help propose solutions. In other cases, you're just going to observe people's language and actions to map them onto a simple change player spectrum.

Mapping people's attitudes, from negative over neutral to positive, on a spectrum is going to be the initial exercise that'll give you a simple visualisation and rough understanding of what are in reality highly complex emotions. It's one of those quick'n'dirty tricks that can indicate where to prioritise your time and attention. If you're in a relatively small organisation and know your people individually, this exercise could be a representation of people's general working attitudes, but always, always, *always* keep an open mind and give people the chance to surprise you, before you (not quite literally) put them in a box. While someone like Kim, who is usually incredibly enthusiastic about learning opportunities, might be feeling mad at the moment about being excluded and is currently giving you a cold shoulder, someone like Chris, who is usually grumpy and disengaged behind a computer, might have had a life-changing event last week that you know nothing about and which is currently leading him to seize every opportunity to give back to the world.

In any case, you need to make it your mission to move people along the spectrum, from negative, via neutral, to positive. Believe me when I say that I've seen some incredible transformations on business change journeys among people and in places where I've least expected them. I'll tell you a secret: those who've had to come a long way, from thinking your project is a complete waste of time to personally seeing and understanding the benefits, will becoming your best advocates.

> *No one tells the story of an extraordinary transformation (or a business change) like a convert.*

Summary

To excite people about your project, you'll need to ensure they are adequately and accurately informed about it and the best way to do this is to engage your change agents – your champions and influencers. To get your message out, you'll need to know where everyone stands in relation to your change project, whether positive, negative or neutral. You can use my Change Player Assessment tool to figure this out.

15

EXERCISES: INFORM

OUR INFORM TOOLS

Over the years, I've noticed that there are several commonalities among the people who are affected by and involved in business change projects. There will be some who will buy into your project instantly, rally for it even; some who will straight up boycott everything; and then some who are somewhere in between and will need something specific from you to successfully adapt. These types all interact with one another and affect each other's state of mind. That's ok, you can work with that, but you do need to know exactly where everyone stands so you can manage it. That's where the Inform tools come in.

Change Player Assessment

Our people spectrum exercise asks you to observe everyone around you, to engage and listen and to empathetically relate to their situations and journeys. You need to get to know your people and put yourself in their shoes. To demonstrate empathy, you need to understand what you can do to help them with the individual difficulties that keep them from successfully adapting to change. This exercise is a way of figuring this out.

I've worked out some broad character type categorisations, with descriptions of general emotions, thoughts and actions for each that will give you an idea of where someone sits on the spectrum. I won't deny that it has taken years to become skilled at honing in, so if you're not feeling confident at reading people, I've created an assessment tool that you can use. To recognise the character types, you and your change agents need to take the following steps:

- Engage with people and listen.

- Tune into your gut feelings.

- Observe the expressions and body language of people when speaking about the change to gauge their true feelings.

- Send out the Change Player Assessment, if you can, or ask people as many of the questions as possible, recording their answers.

- Plot people on the spectrum, according to what you have heard and felt, or use their answers to the fourteen questions asked in the Change Player Assessment.

- With your change agents, plan any additional support that may be required for each type of change player.

You might be wondering how you can plot people's answers based on just gut feeling. The answer is by asking the right questions (and don't forget you can tweak the questions into your own style). You can record their answers – or what you perceive to be the answers – by plotting them on a chart like the one below. From this, you can quickly gauge the overall position of the player you're dealing with, whether more positive (indicated by a 'yes'), negative (indicated by 'no') or neutral (marked as 'not sure').

How do you use the Change Player Assessment to plot people based on their overall scoring? If you're not feeling confident with your own judgements, or maybe the questions aren't flowing for you, why not send your colleagues a questionnaire to fill out? With these fourteen questions, you're transporting yourself back to the '90s and your typical 'Teen Beat' mag. Each question

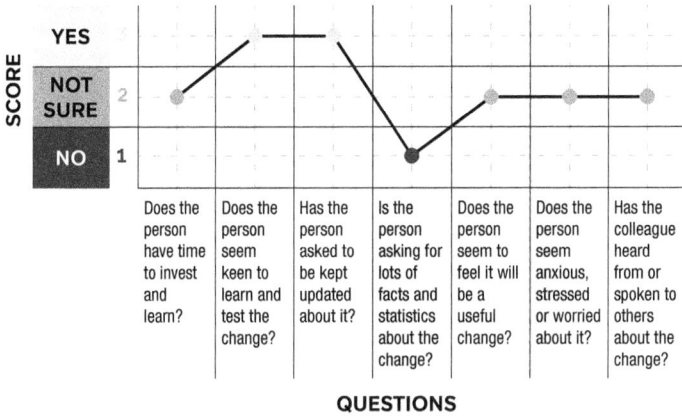

	Does the person have time to invest and learn?	Does the person seem keen to learn and test the change?	Has the person asked to be kept updated about it?	Is the person asking for lots of facts and statistics about the change?	Does the person seem to feel it will be a useful change?	Does the person seem anxious, stressed or worried about it?	Has the colleague heard from or spoken to others about the change?

QUESTIONS

The results from a completed Change Player Assessment revealing that this individual holds a neutral position on the change project

gives a score: 3 for 'yes', 2 for 'not sure', and 1 for 'no'. Add up the scores and then plot the overall total on a plot map and, voila, you have identified your change players. Furthermore, recording all the individual scores on a chart can give a good indication of how a group is feeling as a whole. This information is a great way of opening conversations with senior management about how to tackle teams of change players, and is also a useful exercise to redo later for comparison and to monitor progress.

A plot map detailing the scores from the individual Change Player Assessments provides an overview of how a group of people is feeling

Build, Excite, Equip.

PDF of Change Player Assessment:

BEE Insights tool:

As there are three main types of change player, let's look at each of these in turn.

Positive
Change Player

Positive might sound like this:
- 'You mean I can finally do XYZ?'
- 'About time someone did something!'
- 'Is there anything I can do to lighten the load for you?'
- 'If people used the energy for learning that they are wasting on venting, we would have moved on by now!'
- 'It's not that hard to get, is it?'
- 'What else can I do?'

Positive could sound like this:
- Humour
- Making it no big deal
- Finding the positive and letting it outweigh the negative
- Opening conversations and telling others about the exciting changes, without being asked
- Sitting in the front row during presentations and asking lots of questions

Additional support tactics:
- Encouragement
- Praise
- Recognition
- Gratitude
- Ask them to advocate

Provide additional support to positive change players by:
- Celebrating their success
- Praising their enthusiasm
- Focusing on providing them with up to date, accurate and detailed information
- Letting them lead by example

Negative
Change Player

Negative might sound like this:
- 'What do you mean, I can no longer do XYZ?'
- 'But it's always been done like this!'
- 'Have you read the terrible reviews of this project?'
- 'Have you even done an evaluation of the existing process?'
- 'I'd like to speak to your supervisor.'
- 'Try reaching my kind of tenure here before you tell me what to do!'
- 'Since when do PMs get to tell me how to do my work?'

Negative could sound like this:
- Cynicism or sarcasm
- Offensive language
- Seeking the negative and letting it overshadow the positive
- Encouraging others to reject your project too
- Sharing and spreading their discontent whenever possible
- Sitting in the back row during project presentations (and probably near the snacks; at least they won't leave hungry *and* angry!)

Additional support tactics:
- Support
- Encouragement
- Monitoring
- Give them time to adjust and provide plenty of notice
- Listen, provide perspective
- Provide lots of feedback

Provide additional support to negative change players by:
- Responding to any objections that they may have
- Providing clear communication and easy-to-access support
- Trying to prevent, or at least mitigate the problems that people are likely to experience

Neutral
Change Player

Neutral might sound like this:
- 'I guess'
- 'Probably'
- 'Maybe'
- 'How many meetings do I need to attend, and how many hours of training to I need to make it work?'
- 'Do you think this is really necessary?'
- 'I'm unsure how to do this on top of my work?'
- 'Sign me up if XYZ is in'

Neutral could sound like this:
- Shrugging
- Silence
- Becoming somewhat invisible
- Following their buddies and secret role models
- Sitting somewhere in the middle of the room during project presentations, but positioned off to the side

Additional support tactics:
- Monitor
- Regular contact and updates
- Observe
- Provide statistics
- Ask them to help
- Involve them
- Provide examples of positive colleagues

Provide additional support to neutral change players by:
- Giving them time to adjust to the idea of change
- Providing them with sufficient information (including data, statistics and figures) so that they understand what is happening
- Including them by regularly contacting and updating them

CASE STUDY: RIVER CONSTRUCTION

Ongoing engagement with the change agents at River Construction was crucially important to the success of the project. I wanted to ensure that I had a range of different ways to update and liaise with them, so that they felt confident in my support thereby enabling them to support others.

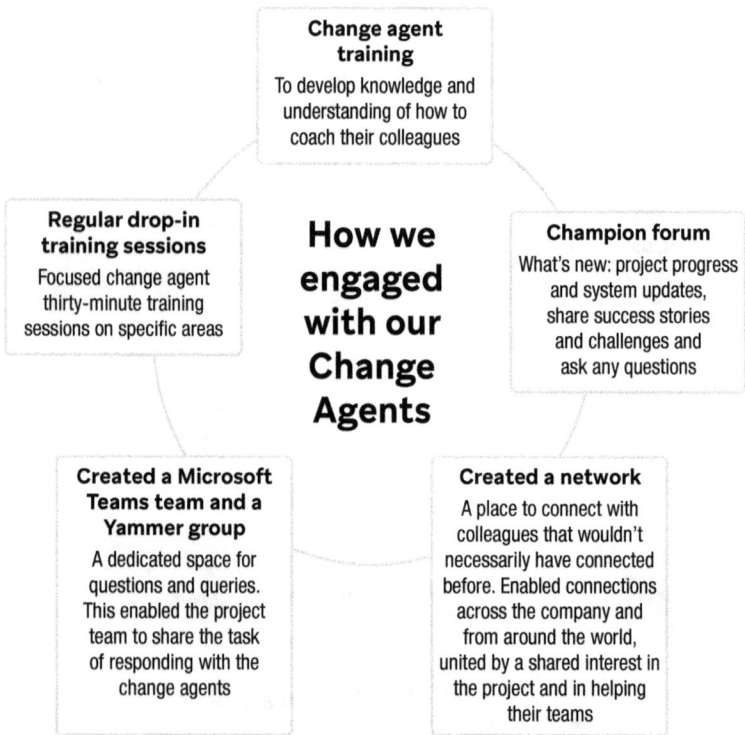

Change agent training
To develop knowledge and understanding of how to coach their colleagues

Regular drop-in training sessions
Focused change agent thirty-minute training sessions on specific areas

How we engaged with our Change Agents

Champion forum
What's new: project progress and system updates, share success stories and challenges and ask any questions

Created a Microsoft Teams team and a Yammer group
A dedicated space for questions and queries. This enabled the project team to share the task of responding with the change agents

Created a network
A place to connect with colleagues that wouldn't necessarily have connected before. Enabled connections across the company and from around the world, united by a shared interest in the project and in helping their teams

The steps taken at River Construction to support the change agents

The change agents worked through the Change Player Assessments with their colleagues, and the results were then marked on a plot map, which gave a clear indication of who held which position. The change agents were then able to focus their attention on those requiring more encouragement, to enable them to increase their scores.

Let us consider the results from the finance department. During the assessments, Rishi, the change agent for Finance, invited his colleagues to fill out the fourteen-question survey that I had provided. After the results were in, Rishi immediately booked one-to-one meetings with those identified as negative change players, Erica, Manuel and Ted, to discuss their specific concerns about the project. He provided Rania, CFO, with the full overview of their team, so that she could congratulate Cass, Sinclair, Ben and Farah on holding a positive position as strong activists for the change. This left the neutral change players to tackle, of which there remained a significant number. With a little encouragement from Rania, Ashton and Mari gradually started becoming more positive towards the project, and when provided with some additional facts and figures, Ruben, Kendall and Kusama also warmed up to the project and became more engaged.

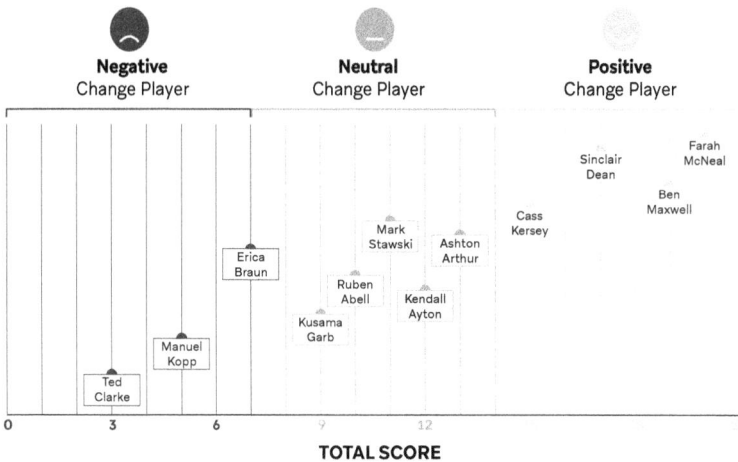

The Change Player Assessment scores for River Construction's finance department

155

16

MARKET

SETTING THINGS IN MOTION

It's finally here. The time to go campaigning for your project. The time to use all your resources to market and sell the change. The time to rally the troops and shout from the rooftops.

You've reached the Market stage of the Excite phase and now you're ready to set your change project in motion. You've been preparing for this new start like NASA with the first moon landing. I've wanted to build up to this point cautiously, with careful explanations and several exercises to work through first, so that you don't fall straight into a 'just go for it' mindset before anyone is actually ready to go for it. Business change is a big thing, and you know that. It's perhaps the biggest transformation your organisation has gone through in the last few years (perhaps ever?), so now is your chance to make this an exciting time, a much-needed challenge, a long-overdue upgrade – or at least a manageable disruption for everyone.

You should by now have all your resources accounted for and lined up to make this business change a reality. You know the quirks of your organisation inside-out, you've really gotten to know the people and you've positioned your project accordingly. Thanks to data collection and social engagement, you should have a pretty good understanding of how things work and what you can do to make this transition to a new status quo happen. Like a true business change manager, you have constructed a change narrative with irrefutable logic, designed a strong project brand identity and matching media package, taken the time to consider how to communicate your ideas with authenticity and heart instead of hiding behind digital convenience, and started building intentional relationships to show those affected by change some real empathy.

You've come a long way. You've systematically covered all three elements necessary to build trust, if you haven't noticed. You now know where you're going and you know who can help you get there, and you have the necessary data to back up your decisions along the way. You've got a team of supporters lined up and ready to smash it – your project team and change agents – and your knowledge platform is fast coming together to educate the people. What I'm trying to tell you is it's all there. You've got this.

Finding a public face

I am now getting to the part where you will need to say stuff out loud, quite literally. Now is a really good time to figure out who's a good public speaker in your inner circle; they might be the right person to deliver the news to the people. While it's always great to see the one who's pulling the strings getting behind the microphone (that would be you...), it might be that having to stand on stage and face a hundred sets of eyes staring back is your biggest nightmare.

Not all of us enjoy the spotlight and not everyone can pull out one crowd-pleasing comment after another, but if you feel up for the challenge, you should absolutely give it a try and get behind that microphone yourself. Remember, if you're tempted but unsure, and you have the time and budget available, you could meet up with a presentation coach a couple of times before the big day to practise and pick up a few tips. It can be terrifying, exciting, frustrating and rewarding all at once to be at the forefront of the campaign; it'll certainly be an extraordinary opportunity to grow in your role as a project manager-turned-business change manager.

If you have a history of going into shock-induced paralysis as soon as collective attention is on you, then please let someone else do the job, otherwise you risk jeopardising the first public outing of your project (and potentially ridiculing everyone who's involved in it). Picking the designated speaker is a strategic decision and it's wise to explore your options thoroughly. However, do be careful that you don't end up dumping the job on someone who wants it even less than you, just because you'd feel more comfortable on the side-lines or (weirdly) enjoy exercising your power as the project leader. This is your project and it is your responsibility to ensure that the people find out about what's going on in the best way possible.

Now that you've thought about who should deliver the news, it's time to revisit your early project communication plans to fine-tune how and when you want to deliver the news. I'm sure that you gave this a good amount of thought during the Build phase, but as the days and weeks have gone by, I'm also sure that things have changed around there and will need to be reassessed before you go up on that stage for the project's first public outing. Get a feel for the general mood at your organisation and how the trusted people in your network (such as the champions and influencers) have been responding to your plans; think about delivery formats that seem appropriate for the current circumstances, and get concrete with dates, times and places. You got this far. Now, get out and market the heck out of this endeavour.

Finding a beginning

I suggest you start by warmly inviting people to join your first public outing. Make it a social event, send out nicely designed invitation letters, come up with incentives for the first X-many people to register, plaster the hallways with posters, install a countdown in the reception area – do anything you can think of that catches people's attention.

Perhaps you can find a little inspiration in the movie industry's approach to marketing the release of a new movie? First, they sneak a little preview into another movie, advertise the movie heavily on TV, creep their way into your social media, hold ridiculously extravagant release parties with celebrities to celebrate – and only then can you finally see the movie yourself. I'm not suggesting you hire a film crew here, I'm just saying that there are ways to build up to an event, and personal invitations, flyers next to the coffee maker and perhaps a few project-coloured M&Ms could be a good start.

> *Make your project visible, and get creative in the process.*

Deciding on the delivery

Your creative thinking should also include the meeting location for your first (and all subsequent) outings. Of course, you can just show up in some open space office and give your big presentation from the dark corner between a fifty-year-old photocopier and a dusty filing cabinet; alternatively, you could make an effort and do something special. Lure people away from their all-day-every-day work settings for a minute to gather them somewhere special that is symbolic of all your excitement; perhaps there's a fancy meeting room that can fit a ton of people but is usually reserved for C-level management only? Perhaps some part of your building has been freshly renovated, which would really suit the story of a fresh start.

> *Space can have an incredible impact on people.*

Do some more of that creative thinking and consider what meeting format would best suit the current mood and circumstances. Instead of just standing up on stage and rattling through your notes, why not add a short panel discussion with a project team member, an influencer and a C-level manager, with you as the moderator? Could you set up a town hall meeting where people can ask questions, opening up the dialogue immediately? If you've got a major business change project at hand that affects loads of people at multiple branches, why not hold a roadshow over several days to meet with them all in person?

Presenting the project – finally

Now on to preparing what it is that you should be including in your presentations. Again, obviously I won't be giving you an exact formula here, but I do recommend that you stick to the front-loading strategy that I introduced earlier in the context of video messages: deliver all the 'need to knows' first, when people's attention is focused, and share the 'nice to knows' later, when people are slowly drifting off.

As the day of your first public outing approaches, refresh your memory of the project mission statement and prepare all the slogans, catchphrases and sales pitches that you can think of. Your project needs to be talked into life, and your strategic messages are going to help you do that (if you manage to get them out without sounding like a robot who was programmed to say just one thing...). What you do and say in the early stage of your campaign can really affect whether people feel that you're doing this for them, not for better numbers or some mysterious performance report.

When the time of the presentation arrives, give a broad introduction to the project in general. Give its title and slogan, show its look and feel (aka the visual design that will be omnipresent from now on), introduce the hard-working project team, the enthusiastic supporters and yourself. Outline the benefits that your product or process brings, the life-saving features, the possibility of work routines becoming a hundred times easier. Point out the problems that you're going to solve with this change and establish a strong sense of 'I need this' among the people.

Inform people, openly and thoroughly, of your plans for them: their anticipated routines under the new status quo, the expectation that they will make use of the digital knowledge platform, the availability of technical and emotional support, and an estimation of when it'll all be over (because switching off the light at the end of the tunnel is always a good move).

Making change digestible

Once you've got this first outing out of the way, start preparing for the smaller meetings with individual divisions, departments and teams, to get into the itineraries for individual learning journeys. While people are now aware that things are about to change, they need clear outlines of what is expected of them. If you think back to the Change Curve, you'll remember that people (perhaps now more than ever) need support to work through a rollercoaster of emotions, which you can respond to in more personal meetings. Take the opportunity of having more intimate meetings to provide a safe space for people to ask questions and air concerns and be sensitive to language and gestures in the process as these might give away where people sit on the broad spectrum of change players.

This is obviously the point where you need a whole lot of help from your project team, your change agents and any formal leaders in the organisational hierarchy with whom you have built strong relationships. In delegating the responsibility to host meetings and explain the new product or process to your supporters, you are starting the process of cutting those apron strings and releasing your change agents, and your project, into the wild. You can probably already sense the loss of control here. What you haven't accounted for, planned and prepared for by now will likely turn into chaos. But then again, you've got everything lined up and ready to go, haven't you?

As you're getting deeper into the campaigning and communicating, gradually add in more of that excitement that you must have been waiting for us to get to. Get louder, bolder, more colourful and confident as you go, growing the whispers of change into an organic roar that has earned its right to existence.

Summary

The Market stage marks the first announcement and public declaration of your change project. It starts with finding the best person to be the public face of your campaign, someone who's a great public speaker and who can tell the story well. It's about creating some buzz around the announcement, finding a fitting time and place to inaugurate your project and then presenting your project with flair. Finally, it's also important to follow up this large public explosion with smaller engagement sessions to make the changes digestible and keep the fires of excitement and expectation burning.

EXCITE PHASE SUMMARY

Transition step: build to excite

○ Prep your communication leads: any people, forums or channels established as part of your communication plans

○ Build relationships with your change agents (the champions and influencers)

○ Understand the Change Curve

Create your strategic marketing campaign

○ Evaluation of Design Capabilities

○ Project Visual Identity Checklist

○ Campaign Kit Checklist

○ 'What's in it for me?' (WIIFM) Video Checklist

○ Key Message Checklist

○ Knowledge Platform Checklist

Know your Change Players

○ Complete your Change Player Assessments

○ Prepare support materials and engagement tactics

Set things in motion

○ Choose your spokesperson/s

○ Revisit your communication plans

○ Organise your first event

○ Present your project

PART IV
EQUIP

Equip

Develop | Educate | Invigorate

17

THE EQUIP PHASE
POWER TO THE PEOPLE

Entering the Equip phase means getting people up to speed and ready to start operating the new product or process by enhancing their digital skills. This idea sounds deceptively simple – *it's just bumping people's skills up a notch, right?* – but this phase is about to become the most exhausting and challenging phase so far. Until now, you have been orchestrating and delegating ever so diligently, but entering Equip means being mentally prepared for things suddenly going in a million different directions, because you are no longer the sole person in charge. The ultimate responsibility for making this business change work is now going to be handed over to the people themselves.

Whether they will choose (or simply 'happen', even) to cultivate the necessary skills to master the change is now out of your control. Once you have got to the point of handing over responsibility, all you can do is make sure that you keep an open line of communication and that people have access to all the resources they could possibly need to pull this off, including an incredibly well-curated and glitch-free knowledge platform and a strong peer support network based around the champions and influencers. I trust that you are getting a strong sense right this moment of how important your tireless preparation efforts over the last days, weeks and months have been? Without knowing how things work at your organisation, without involving those who people trust most, without making a strong marketing case for your project, and without a technical solution that lets people learn in a million different ways, you'd now be standing there empty-handed. But you're not. You came prepared.

What is the Equip phase?

When I say 'equip', what I ultimately mean is providing people with the practical tools and step-by-step manuals to get their jobs done, whether that be simple PDFs or handouts, online formats like recorded video tutorials, or through in-person training such as demonstrations or mentoring sessions. Anything is possible, anything that your people need to get through this. The Equip phase is when you **Develop**, **Educate** and **Invigorate** the change process.

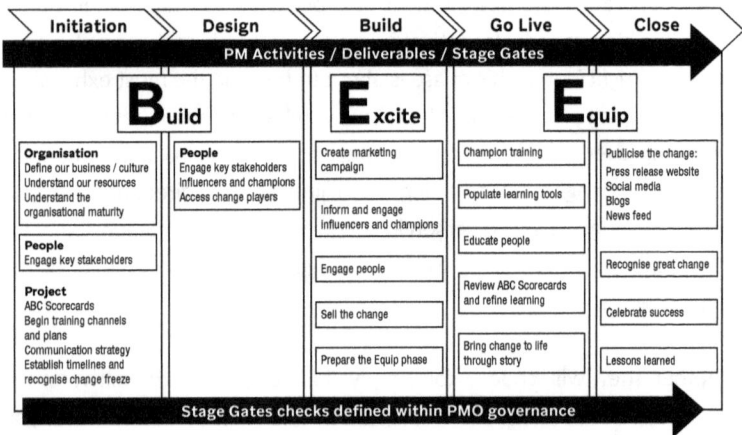

Initiation	Design	Build	Go Live	Close
PM Activities / Deliverables / Stage Gates				
Build		**E**xcite	**E**quip	
Organisation Define our business / culture Understand our resources Understand the organisational maturity	**People** Engage key stakeholders Influencers and champions Access change players	Create marketing campaign	Champion training	Publicise the change: Press release website Social media Blogs News feed
		Inform and engage influencers and champions	Populate learning tools	
People Engage key stakeholders			Educate people	
		Engage people		Recognise great change
Project ABC Scorecards Begin training channels and plans Communication strategy Establish timelines and recognise change freeze		Sell the change	Review ABC Scorecards and refine learning	Celebrate success
		Prepare the Equip phase	Bring change to life through story	Lessons learned
Stage Gates checks defined within PMO governance				

How Build, Excite and Equip can overlay your project framework

In the Equip phase you will:

- Train your change champions

- Create the necessary training tools and materials, including videos, guides, walk-throughs and manuals

- Educate people

- Review your ABC Scorecards and refine individual learning journeys

- Bring the change to life through stories, including interviews, blogs, podcasts and case studies

- Recognise great change

- Celebrate success

- Assess the project after completion and the lessons learned

Maintaining perspective

There's a ton of stuff to consider when it comes to equipping people with new skills. However, please read this chapter with three things in mind:

- You are a project manager-turned-change manager, not a professional trainer. You can encourage and support people by giving them access to resources and further help but personally providing that training is a whole different business.

- Ultimately, your goal is to get everyone in your organisation to full competency in relation to the new product or process. Any move that you make, any learning material you share and any information you send out should reflect that.

- This book only provides a light overview on helping people along their learning journeys. If the transition becomes extremely cumbersome and you're running out of resources to help, hire a professional trainer to get back on track. *Do it, seriously.*

While I'm certainly not suggesting holding every single person's hand throughout the entire process (that would be impossible), I do encourage you to follow closely what's going on, both personally and with the help of your change agents and project team, to get a sense of where people might be on the Change Curve and the people change spectrum. This allows you to determine who might be fine with a self-directed online course in this phase as opposed to those who might need a little more personal attention to stay on track with your project schedule. You don't want people to get stuck in the fear pit, remember?

Before I get into the hands-on aspects of equipping people, let's have a quick look at your project from a perspective that you might not yet have considered.

The politics of learning

When introducing business change, as you are doing now (or perhaps in the near future), it's good to consider digital skills and learning not just in the isolated context of your project, but as part of a much bigger picture. What you're doing here is developing people's abilities and confidence in the technical dimensions of the corporate landscape; this will not only benefit your project but will also prove a major motivation and driver for employees to join and stay with your organisation. This is a 'two bird and one stone' kind of situation. Organisations need their people to learn, but people also need their organisations to care for learning.

When 'the vast majority of CEOs are somewhat or very concerned about the lack of digital skills in their workforce,'[36] as reported by the Boston Consulting Group, then you are in a pretty powerful position to start the conversation about L&D at your organisation, and even drive it up the hierarchy to those who do the strategic decision making. Organisations without designated L&D teams need people like you to take the initiative and incorporate learning into the business agenda. The Boston Consulting Group even suggests 'linking business goals directly to skill-building plans' which, although you're not wiring the whole strategy for the entire organisation (yet?), you are already doing to some degree if your project goals are properly reflected in the ABC Scorecards. In any case, always remember the strategic importance of organisational learning and how your project constitutes a L&D endeavour, particularly if you need a little personal involvement from your senior managers for help in the Invigorate stage. Use the rich potential of learning as your political leverage.

Learning is not just important to the organisation; the matter of learning is equally important to the people, as I said. The *2018 Workplace Learning Report* from LinkedIn found that '94% of employees would stay at a company longer if it invested in their career development' – which is a pretty compelling statistic.[37] I don't want to suffocate you with numbers but the same report also shows that 68% of employees prefer to learn at work, 58% prefer to learn at their own pace, and 49% prefer to learn at the point of need. These are key observations to consider when constructing your learning curriculum and the knowledge platform. You need to create individual learning pathways based on people's areas of application that allow them to engage as intensely as they wish and at a time that suits. You need to hand over control of how people learn to the people themselves, because that's deeply personal business, but you can make dang sure that they are given the time they need to learn by their line managers, team captains or whoever, and that they have easy access, from any device, to the resources on the knowledge platform at an instant.

The creation of learning pathways and the development of an effective knowledge platform are the two things that will determine the success of this last and most crucial phase. While you may already be an expert at the technical execution of these key developments (and if not, you've probably hired one...), I've still got a little more insight of my own to pass on as to how to go about equipping people.

> The golden rules are cutting people some slack in this time of transition and providing ready access to a watertight and intuitive search function.

Different ways of learning

There are loads of theories out there that deal with people's different ways of learning. While they're surely all worthwhile reads should you ever have an idle weekend, I'd rather get straight to the point: people have different ways of processing information and different ways of getting things done. That means that you can't just provide one type of learning material and expect everyone in your organisation to be equally satisfied.

Some people are visual learners who prefer images and graphs over large bodies of text, whereas others may feel exactly the opposite; some might want to listen to learning materials rather than looking at or watching them, while others might need a personal explanation in a dialogical exchange, or indeed a combination of any of the above. You get the gist: it goes a million different ways.

I'm telling you this, not because I suggest you burn through £100K developing the best blended learning platform the world has ever seen, but because I'd like you to consider these differences in learning processes and ensure that your learning materials are a little more diverse than simply a library of plain written text.

Think of places where you can provide step-by-step instructions with infographics or a series of screenshots that make the explanations easier to understand. We all know that a picture is worth a thousand words, so it would be foolish not to remember that when creating the learning materials. If you're feeling really fancy, include audio recordings so that people can navigate the new interface as they listen to instructions, and provide video tutorials for the more complicated tasks. Give people the opportunity to participate in in-person coaching events if they'd like (and, well, if your budget allows for it). Also consider setting up a progress interface, so that people get an idea of where they are on their learning journey and can therefore plan their time appropriately. How about integrating a no-risk test space within the knowledge platform, where people can play around and try things out without breaking anything?

You may have noticed that this isn't exactly rocket science. Creating a diverse collection of learning materials is simply a matter of employing a bit of creativity and resourcefulness to work with what you have, while also pushing the boundaries at the same time. Now is not the same time to do things only as 'they've always been done', so consider if there are new methods of conveying information or alternative channels that you could explore? Think about your own media consumption habits, noticing the high expectation that we all have these days to be able to choose between videos, podcasts, newsletters and so on and so forth whenever we are taking in information.

Equipping, not dictating

The most important point I want to make is this: even if you provide everybody with the same set of learning materials that instruct them to do things in a certain way, you're never going to end up a with a team of robots who all do exactly what you want them to do in the way that you want them to do it.

You are equipping people with the resources to figure this thing out themselves so that it can best complement their way of working. You are giving them learning materials that outline a possible route if they want to get from A to B, but I promise you they'll find new ways and routes that you haven't even considered, because your focus has been on planning the transition. Remember that you are only facilitating people's initial steps – familiarisation, acceptance and adoption of the product or process – you're not the one to dictate or judge how they'll eventually end up using it. Please don't forget that you have a whole bunch of clever and experienced people sitting behind your organisation's computer screens – people who are extremely good, if not full-on experts, at doing their own jobs and managing their work lives independently. They don't need micromanaging. Think of it as artistic freedom.

Think of all the different routes that people take to reach the new status quo as a source of inspiration and insight in themselves. As I've said before, this stage is about simply facilitating and handing the responsibility over to the people.

One more thing...

There's a little bit of housekeeping left. I know you're desperate to get going and start getting your hands dirty by working with the new product or process at last, but this bit is absolutely critical if you want this phase to work on a tight schedule. To do this, you'll need to start planning times and co-ordinating calendars right about now, even though you won't be executing these activities until the Coach stage. You are going to need to ensure you have all hands on deck, so if you want your project team, champions, influencers and, last but not least, your charismatic CEO to be around when the transition happens, you need to impose an immediate holiday freeze on everyone's calendars. A simple note to HR, an announcement during the next change agent meeting and a calendar invite to those involved will do. It is up to you whether you make the transition period a time of company-wide holiday freeze or if you require only those with a direct function in your project to be around. Whatever you decide, stick with it and don't budge at the first extraordinary request. This time is important to the health of your organisation and commitment is non-negotiable.

Summary

The Equip phase is about skilling people up to make them experts in the new system, product or process. There are three stages:

- **Develop:** Create training materials and train champions.

- **Educate:** Train people innovatively and refine that learning.

- **Invigorate:** Bring change to life through stories and case studies.

18

DEVELOP

KNOWLEDGE PLATFORM AND CHANGE AGENTS

The Develop stage of the Equip phase that we're entering now is about two developmental processes that happen in parallel. One is the development of your knowledge platform, including a strict and unwavering use of your brand identity, and the creation of the learning materials in a variety of different formats; the other is the promotion and growth of your change agents' skills, including enhancing their understanding of the new product or process as well as their skills in disseminating that knowledge to the people they're supporting. In other words, you're about to start intensively growing the two essential resources on which the success of the next stage rests (FYI, that's when you'll finally start coaching people).

The development of the knowledge platform is super important at this stage because you want people to get a great first impression of your new product or process. They need to have a convincing and persuasive experience when they start accessing the learning materials that show them what the new thing can do and how it's better than the existing solution. You also want them to feel safe and adequately challenged as they navigate the different sections, explore the various components and work through the exercises that will help develop new working routines.

Developing your change agents' skills is critical at this point because it will become crucially important that they know their way around the new product or process. Someone has to practise what you preach, know where you are headed and lead by good example. Your change champions and influencers are the first target group to be exposed to the new product or process. Make them feel as important as the members of an exclusive membership club or the VIPs to your show; their excitement, confidence and enthusiasm should spread among the social clusters at your organisation. The better they understand, the better they can promote the product or process, and persuade and support their peers.

Despite these two developmental processes going in two completely different directions – one is purely technological and the other is as human as it gets – they're still closely related and intertwined with one another. They have the same aspiration at their foundation, that of moving people towards transition and getting them ready for go-live. They are both efforts to support, enable and reinforce people's learning processes. I therefore suggest you consider a number of questions and allow your answers to guide you through the Develop stage, as they give you a distinct view on the needs of others. Not your project's needs. Not your KPIs' crying demands. Be guided purely and simply by the needs of your people.

For each of these developmental processes, ask yourself these questions:

1. Who is learning?

2. What will they be learning?

3. What do they need to learn?

4. How will they learn?

5. How will they maintain what they have learned?

For the sake of your project planning and KPI requirements, there is one additional question:

6. By what date should they have reached their learning goals?

From here on out, whether you're working on developing the knowledge platform or preparing your champions and influencers for their job as peer leaders, these six questions should be at the heart of your thinking and doing.

To provide a little more guidance on how to answer these questions (rather than just throwing them at you and crossing my fingers), let's look at them in closer detail in the context of your knowledge platform and the prep work with your change agents. One thing though: the last question is totally specific to your own project and I'm confident that you can figure that out yourself.

Developing the knowledge platform

In Part III, I introduced the knowledge platform as a single location for all resources relevant to the business change, that people can access anywhere, anytime and on their device of choice, not only to undertake formal training but also to find quick solutions and answers to urgent questions as they arise. It should be set up to meet current UX design standards to assure accessibility, intuitive use and support a goal-oriented learning journey.

I want you now to start populating this platform with project-specific information, guidance, short lessons and targeted exercises that help people get acquainted with the new product or process. Begin thinking of it as an online classroom and a digital library, a single learning environment where those affected by and involved in the business change can gradually build their knowledge of the new product or process through their autonomous and self-guided efforts. Obviously, this means one thing: it all needs to be totally self-explanatory. One hundred percent – and even more, if possible.

Knowledge platforms ('resource knowledge centres' to some) are a common way to share information on a particular subject. Many organisations use custom-built websites or web-based collaboration platforms to collect and display webinars, instructional PDFs, relevant case studies and other materials that are linked together in a logical fashion and with a straightforward menu structure – a one-stop shop for insights, information and updates on your project.

Before you get carried away and start building this resource from scratch, I recommend first searching for existing resources to avoid reinventing the wheel. A good place to start is by looking at your supplier's website and available materials: if they have had the confidence and creativity to invent a genuinely innovative solution for your industry's problems, it seems likely that they will also have created a stack of materials to help a new user navigate their product. Chances are they even had a significant chunk of cash at their disposal for this task, which you probably don't, so make use of what is freely available to you.

Your knowledge platform is the critical tool in scaling this massive learning effort. You obviously can't introduce everyone personally to what's new and what's cool, but you can put a system in place that helps you record recurrent searches and frequently accessed materials. This will help you to understand what people are prioritising and where they struggle on their journey, to target your approach accordingly. Some designers even go the extra mile and gamify the whole thing with quizzes and personal challenges; this is something that I clearly see working particularly well in the sort of mobile applications that people have become so worryingly addicted to.

But now, on to a consideration of the questions I posed earlier.

1. Who is learning?

This could be everyone in your organisation, within a particular division, a selection of departments or an individual team. This might involve people in two time zones or ten, a handful or in the order of thousands, working from corporate offices or their homes, English as a first or as an additional language. You need to know these distinctions so that you can target your learning material most appropriately.

A look at the Corporate Survey conducted in the Build phase will help provide a broad overview (see Chapter 6), but taking it a step further, try to understand more about the actual people behind the rather resource-focused anonymous survey. Are they part of a younger or an older demographic? Are they tech-savvy or tech-averse? Do they feel confident that they can keep up with the changes? A look at the Organisation Assessment from the Build phase can provide insight here (see Chapter 6). While you won't be able to smooth the path individually for every single person at your organisation, you can certainly be mindful of the tendencies exposed in your data (since you've already collected it anyway).

2. What will they be learning?

Your users will need specific, targeted and focused information that is appropriate and pertinent to their particular roles. However, there is still a baseline knowledge of the new product or process that everyone will need to achieve to perform generic tasks. That includes, for example, the log-in process, navigation of the new dashboard and the specific vocabulary used in operation. Every user will need a solid grasp of these foundational skills if they are to use the new product or process appropriately.

While there will be distinct differences in which features will be of particular interest to people from specific departments (for example, those working in Accounts will have different learning needs from those working in Marketing), there is also likely to be a distinction between different groups of employees and their user authority. The managers will have different levels of access to product features from the general employees and may use completely different areas of the product or process. Develop the knowledge platform in a way that starts their learning journeys with generic knowledge and then try sending people down more targeted and tailored paths that reflect their individual positions and responsibilities within the organisation.

3. What do they need to learn?

Be extremely practical here. Don't turn this question into some philosophical exercise on knowledge acquisition, but instead list the kinds of tasks that you expect people to perform by the time go-live comes around. For example, when introducing a new collaboration software, stipulate that people need to be able to create new files, share them with team members, edit and export them as Microsoft Word documents and PDF files and locate them in the folder structure afterwards. This list of required skills will obviously vary depending on the product or process you're introducing, but try to be painfully specific here.

This exercise may come across as ridiculously trivial but believe me when I say that having clear expectations works wonders when it comes to the learning process and people's expectations of themselves and others.

4. How will they learn?

This is the big, big question. How oh how will I help people learn what they need to know to be ready to work once the new solution goes live? Again, remember that you're not a certified trainer or qualified teacher. But you are a subject expert who can share your knowledge in a variety of formats. You just need to know which to choose.

There are various methods that you can use to convey your knowledge and expertise to others. These can include, but are not at all limited to:

- Videos, ideally short and to the point, so that people can easily watch in their own time

- Podcasts, which can be done as engaging videos or simple audio files

- Live webinars, perhaps as a hybrid of expert presentation and interactive Q&A session

- Classroom sessions with a subject expert (or even a professional trainer, should that turn out to be necessary)

- Detailed manuals with in-depth explanations, illustrations/ photographs/screenshots, and PDF guides as a quick access version with step-by-step instructions

- A 24-7 online Q&A channel where people can get in touch for help

- Community engagement so people can support others

5. How will they maintain what they have learned?

Another great question. Retention comes from repetition, incorporation of the new skills or knowledge into the existing work routine and reinforcement of the individual transition success.

One way to encourage and promote retention is to use digital prompts to remind people of product features they haven't used or tasks they haven't performed in a while. A nudge can be a personalised email, an instant message or a pop-up window on the knowledge platform that prompts a person to take a specific action or reminds them to practise something they haven't done in a while.

Developing the skills of the change agents

Equipping your people is the main purpose of this phase, and it begins right here with the champions and influencers; your change agents (from the human perspective) now need to be trained up to become your super-users – the technical side of their role. These are the people who will drive your project forward among their peers so you need to ensure that they are sufficiently skilled to do so. They need to know the product inside out, upside down, off the top of their heads and with a confidence resembling that of a circus artist on a tightrope. They need to feel and convey a level of genuine commitment and expertise that radiates through the corridors in a way that makes others excited to jump on the bandwagon and come along for the ride.

To make this as clear as possible: your champions and influencers need to develop technical expertise on the one hand and a degree of mindfulness towards people on the other hand. Only when they know the new product or process intimately can they become attuned to people's individual journeys along the Change Curve and their positions as change players. This requires a whole lot of care and consideration on both their part and yours, perhaps more than ever before, but there's no doubt in my mind: together you can achieve anything.

One golden rule though: there needs to be super-special treatment of your change agents. They really deserve it.

Now, back to business, answering the same five questions posed above.

1. Who is learning?

The answer is the people whose support you absolutely need the most. The people who are on board with the change already and willing to dedicate their time and energy towards the success of your project. The people who have a good knowledge of the workings of your organisation and accurate gut feelings when it comes to the people and what needs to be done. This is high-level stuff.

Most importantly, don't forget the people on your organisation's support teams, like the IT desk and the L&D centre.

2. What will they be learning?

The answer to this is two-fold, as mentioned above. They need to learn both the new product or process (the generic baseline knowledge as well as an even spread of the niche knowledge required by specific departments or teams), and a little bit of people stuff on how to handle, lead, guide and support people. This needs to include an introduction to the concepts of the Change Curve, the change players and the people spectrum, because the change agents will need to be able to 'read' people in these terms.

3.   What do they need to learn?

As with developing the knowledge platform, your answer to this question needs to be painfully specific. Because their current job description is to help others make sense of why on earth they should bother, the change agents should be able to position the role of the individual within the bigger picture. They will need to know many different facets of the new product or process and understand how it's to be used within, between and across teams, departments and the whole organisation.

An additional perspective to consider here is how they should respond and act in critical situations. As the project leader, you need to work out a set of possible responses and actions (a protocol, if you will) to serve as guidelines for when the change agents are working on the floor in real-life scenarios. What should they do if employees portray complete desperation or go into a state of outright refusal? What should they do if someone is so enthusiastic about the business change that they want to help too? When should they call in help? When do they need to consult you?

4.   How will they learn?

I'll come right out and say it: your change agents can't be kept at an arm's length or be put through some boring, detached online training on the subject. These people carry a burden so critical to your project's success that they need to be treated like royalty.

You need to build strong bonds between your change agents, and between them and you. You will need to gather them in person – or remotely if that works better – in a setting as special as your budget allows, to give them a strong sense of belonging, pride and purpose. Make them feel thoroughly appreciated and remind them that they are about to learn from an outstanding technical expert (yes, that can be you if you're up for the job) and someone who is exceptionally proficient in the people stuff, such as empathy, leadership and the like.

5.   How will they maintain what they have learned?

Don't think that one short day of training is enough to equip your change agents with all the technical expertise and emotional intelligence they need to fulfil their duties and meet your ongoing expectations. As you do with all people impacted by the change, you need to make a continuing effort for you and the project to be visible and seen, constantly creating opportunities for them to meet and discuss what's going on; this is particularly true with high-profile people like your change agents, the ones on which you – and the success of the project – rely so heavily. They'll need your help and each other's support to tackle any problems and crack the transition; their greatest opportunity to consolidate collective knowledge and cultivate the strength they need to get through this time of change lies in these dialogues and exchanges. This is also a great moment to instil a healthy feedback culture to continue gathering vital information as to where people are struggling so that you can continue to build support resources to overcome any potential hurdles. I'm well aware that this is another big task and probably completely new territory for you, but you've made it this far and you've learned a whole lot along the way. This, too, is doable.

Remember that you're not alone: I'm sure that there are a ton of people in your organisation who are experts in these fields and more than willing to share their expertise and knowledge – you just have to ask.

CASE STUDY: RIVER CONSTRUCTION

At River Construction, I knew that for our change agents to support and help others they needed to be adequately trained in all the different areas that are important for our project. This training was provided to the change agents first, before they began their engagement with the wider team, to help them understand their role so that they could support me in cascading the message going forward.

This preparation included not only system training, but also instruction on how they could successfully support others. It was delivered through a variety of webinars, bitesize WIIFM videos and PDF guides, and covered the following topics:

- What are 'change agents' – their attributes, roles and responsibilities

- How change agents can help

- Understanding fear responses and the Change Curve

- Introduction to concept of the change players

- How to engage with the different types of change players

- How to be a good coach

- Product-specific benefits

- In-depth product training

I created this training syllabus, along with a number of support channels and networks, as part of our change agent engagement programme, which together equipped them to feel confident in their positions as change agents.

Good Coaches
The best coaches don't tell, they encourage and support someone to seek the answers for themselves. This is the way we learn quickly.

Ask questions and guide them to find their own solution

Support and encourage them

Confirm their understanding

Praise them for their successes

Summary

The Develop stage has two prongs: establishing the knowledge platform, and developing your change agents. Both these things can be achieved by answering the same set of questions which revolves around the 'who', 'what', 'why' and 'how' of these skills.

19

EDUCATE

GIVING PEOPLE
WHAT THEY NEED

By this stage, you have hopefully (well, 'ideally' really...) constructed a spectacular edifice of a knowledge platform, and figured out how to endow your change agents with the knowledge and skills they need to help you bring this change to the masses. All in good time – *but I suspect also not without a fair amount of 'constructive' stress and 'valuable' pressure. It's the nature of the business, my friend.*

Naturally, you're now desperate to move on to the moment where the magic finally happens and your project dream becomes an organisation-wide reality – go-live – but before that can happen, every single person who will have anything to do with the new product or process has to learn how to use it. This is what the Educate stage of the Equip phase is all about. Let the learning begin.

You're undeniably an expert in the subject area and there's probably nobody within your organisation who knows more about the new product or process than you do (congratulations on that...), but it's important that you don't confuse your expertise and enthusiasm with your qualifications.

It might be useful here to get a better understanding of what the difference between a coach and a trainer is exactly, so that you know what I'm asking you to do – and not do – at this stage. This is a valuable exercise in any case, as the line between one and the other can sometimes be blurred and you can find yourself doing a bit of both roles. If this happens, it's extremely important that you know when you have reached the limit of what you can do for your people and can recognise the need to call in a professional trainer for help.

First, let's talk training

I don't want to repeat myself here, but I will: professional training is a skill in itself and its importance should never, ever be underestimated in any change project. Ever. *Did I say never ever?*

It is likely that you have already analysed your people's training needs when you were navigating yourself through the Build phase and bringing together your project plans. Like any good project manager, you have probably put a healthy budget forecast in your plans, to fund an army of professional trainers all primed and ready to create the training materials and training sessions needed to support the people.

Now you are likely to face what my years of experience have shown to be perhaps the greatest challenges faced by project teams organising training: attendance. No matter how good your training, or how cleverly constructed or how conveniently timed or located, people just don't tend to come.

There is little more frustrating in the world of projects than this common dialogue:

> **Project Team:** So, Business Colleague, why have you not embraced the new system?

> **Business Colleague:** I don't know how to use the system, no one has shown me.

Project Team: We have provided training every Tuesday and drop-in lunch sessions, plus there is a 24-7 support channel where you can access help at any time. You might also have noticed the Training Team floor-walking during the go-live, wearing the glowing neon t-shirts?

For my next point, I want to first ask forgiveness from my dear training colleagues, as you are totally awesome and this is not to be taken as a personal criticism; like all observational comedy sketch shows, what I am about to say is, in fact, based on typical human behaviour.

While there is absolutely a need for the ongoing provision of training sessions in all their richness, project teams also know that change leaders need to support trainers more... *and the way training is delivered needs to change.*

We live in a fast-moving and digitally evolving world, where people are continually working beyond capacity and yet still they are constantly being bombarded with endless changes and challenges that disrupt their working lives. It's therefore time for project teams (yes, that includes the trainers as part of the team) to think about more inventive and ingenious ways to 'sell' the training to their people. We need to find innovative ways of communicating the training available; allocating the resources for one-to-one sessions to specific individuals (of course, you'll know this now as part of your training analysis from Build); developing effective but engaging self-learning materials, employing fresh gamification (see BEE: Interact, Chapter 20) and learning pathway analysis. All of this is, of course, showcased in your knowledge platform that also doubles up as the go-to communication hub.

Here, in a nutshell, is how to develop an effective training team plan:

During the Build phase:

1. Allocate training resource to the project.

2. Work with the trainer to understand your audience and their learning requirements.

3. Start compiling and developing the training plans and materials, ensuring a wide variety of formats as well as content. Think about what can be sourced from the suppliers' existing materials and what additional resources you may require. Who might need dedicated one-to-one training? *Note: sometimes this works wonders for promotion too.*

4. Where possible, try to get senior stakeholders to agree to make training mandatory, often pushed through via a learning management system; take tips from your Health and Safety (H&S) department – they're super good at ensuring you are complying with their safety requirements. Even some cleverly crafted wording merely suggesting or implying 'mandatory' can go a long way...

5. Allocate more budget to the ongoing provision and development of the training materials.

What 'open resource' training materials are already available online? You may find you just need to direct colleagues to these, highlighting that some of the features may differ slightly.

During the Excite phase:

1. Highlight the knowledge platform as part of your campaign, emphasising that all updates will be posted here and training can be booked from here.

2. Develop some out-of-the-box training materials, unleashing your creativity and playful side.

3. Begin building excitement around the training programme you are planning.

4. Draw in your change agents, allowing them to support the development process and using their influence to encourage their teams to sign-up for training.

During the Equip phase:

1. Go to town with the plans.

2. Get those champions trained and book the one-to-one training sessions to help with future attendance.

3. Ensure your training team is reporting frequently on attendance levels and be sure to seek support from your influencers when levels are lower than expected, hoped for or needed.

Training versus coaching

I have discussed training and the importance of employing training experts when appropriate. Now it is time to cover coaching and consider how you personally can focus on this area, while trainers are doing their thing. Imagine an occasion when you may not have the budget for a trainer; or perhaps there is a group of negative change players who won't attend or engage with training. If this is the case, you may need to introduce coaching, as well as, or perhaps instead of, the training; either way, this should have been recognised as part of your Build phase activities and therefore anticipated.

Let us start by establishing clear and straightforward definitions for 'coaching' and 'training', and then explore the distinction between the two in a way that I think anyone without a university major in psychology or pedagogics can get behind.

Training is aimed at the development of a particular skill with the purpose of improvement; it is 'knowledge transfer at scale' and focused on accomplishing certain routinised behaviours.[38]

Coaching is about enhancing skills and knowledge through one-on-one access to a person with experience; it often builds on the skills obtained through training, developing it with tips, tricks and hints to the point where it can be applied in an informed and creative way in practice.[39]

The same people at the 'learning innovation company' Maestro also came up with this little table that compares various aspects of training and coaching to make clear their differences; obviously this is something that I don't want to keep from you.

The table below gives you an example of how Training and Coaching differ, including approach

	Training	Coaching
Aim	Transferring knowledge	Enhancing knowledge or skills
Settings	Often used in group setting	Usually one-on-one
Location	Frequently off-site or at a special facility	Usually on-the-job
Target	Often used for new hires	More often used with experienced employees
Approach	Usually structured	Usually unstructured
Atmosphere	Formal	Informal, conversational
Format	Depends on telling	Depends on asking
Focus	Learning-focused	Development-focused

In summary, a trainer provides standardised, subject-oriented knowledge and instructions with a view to specific tasks or jobs, while a coach is a relationship-oriented supporter who assists with reflection and attitude towards tasks and jobs. Within your project, both roles are present, to be shared between you and your change agents.

In your project, with the technical guidance provided by your super-useful knowledge platform, people can take on the role of trainers-to-themselves by acquiring knowledge and developing new practices in their own time and through their own efforts. You and your group of change agents act as coaches who help people to understand the meta perspective of why this transition makes sense. This doesn't mean that you can't show Alex from PR how to set up a new workflow step-by-step; it just means that you're not qualified to tell everyone exactly how to do their jobs, and the onus is on the individual to obtain the necessary skills and expertise, with the assistance of the various support structures that have been put in place.

There's just one promise that I will ask you to make, to me, to your people and to yourself. If you sense that things are not moving forward or that the working atmosphere at your organisation is getting increasingly sour because people are having a hard time with the transition, you need to promise that you will hire in a professional trainer who is specialised in your new product or process. In a dangerous situation like that, where the entire success of the project is at risk, you can be a coach and work with people on values and attitudes as much as you want but it won't make a difference, and will probably even make things worse. I call this the Ripcord Promise: you are committing to honesty with yourself and others, and rather than let the project crash to the ground, you'll pull the ripcord and bring in additional help.

The Coach 1.0 Cycle: How to coach the people

Now that we're all on the same page about the purpose and remits of coaching (wonderful), let's look at what it is about in terms of content.

The coaching element of your role is where you get those affected by the change ready to roll, people like Kim from Marketing, Ahmad from Customer Service, Neela from HR, Vic and Charlie from Accounts, Nicky from IT and Billie from Operations. This is the stage where you support them on their learning journeys so that they can eventually navigate the new product or process confidently and integrate it into their everyday work routines with ease. You want to help prepare them to reach the point where they feel comfortable to transition into a new status quo (remember the Change Curve?). In other words, this stage is all about facilitating learning. In addition, and this is said not to alarm you but just to keep you on your toes, you are edging ever closer to the moment when you will move your index finger to that big red button and push it real good, releasing the new product or process into the wild.

Summary

The Educate stage of the Equip phase is all about ensuring that every person in the organisation who needs to use the new system knows how to do so. You can achieve this through training or coaching, or a combination of both.

20

EXERCISES: EDUCATE
OUR EDUCATE TOOLS

To be clear about what needs to happen next, and to help you stay on course with your adventure, I've divided the necessary actions from this point into three periods: before, during and after your new product or process has gone live. You should be able to just pick up a pen and check them off like boxes on a to-do list; they're pretty self-explanatory and probably on your radar already. These are mostly administrative tasks and not always directly related to your role as a coach. Perhaps they need to become part of your trainer's role, if you have one, but remember that the underlying mindset matters in everything you do from now on as it can help in weaving people and process together.

BEE: Interact

To help you transition smoothly through the Educate stage of Equip, I suggest that you use my BEE: Interact tools. BEE: Interact is my own product-specific adoption website offering innovative games and inventive solutions to provide fun, engaging, out of the norm training that helps excite people as they learn. This enables successful product adoption to be delivered remotely and at scale in an enjoyable and engaging manner, embedding knowledge while also keeping them up to date with ongoing changes in the product.

Checklist 1: What to do before go-live

There are quite a few things to remember before your new product or process goes live. Don't be intimidated by what might seem a rather long list of tasks, they are just reminders to do the small things that make a big difference. Before go-live, these are the tasks that must be completed:

- Ensure that your knowledge platform is ready (in both functionality/content).

- Activate a no-risk playground within the new product or process for people to try it out.

- Set up a support channel on your organisation's communication platform.

- Provide everyone in the organisation with access to the knowledge platform and ensure that everyone can log on and use it.

- Announce the beginning of the collective learning journey.

- Widely display your excitement and enthusiasm, in person and via the change agents, about kick-off to try and kindle it in others.

- Have your supporters (this could be a team of change agents and project team members) walk the hallways, and be accessible and immediately available to help people on demand.

- Host exhibition-style information sessions in the canteen or courtyard.

- Send daily prompts and notifications with a 'Task of the Day' or highlighting a special feature.

- Analyse your platform statistics to see what content people are accessing frequently and where people might be struggling.

- Adjust functionality and content accordingly.

- Meet your change agents regularly to discuss issues and progress.

You and your change agents are no longer simply holding hands, uttering encouragement and sweet-talking people into getting on board with the change. You are actively getting busy, explaining and justifying the change to peers; introducing the knowledge platform to those who will take responsibility for their own learning; talking through and demonstrating the features and functions to those who perhaps won't be so proactive; taking mental notes on people's places on the spectrum of change player, and mindfully moving everyone along the Change Curve. You see, technical expertise and people stuff matter equally.

One clever thing you can do here to lighten the load for your change agents, if you've still got planning capacity, is introducing the concept of 'tandem running'. The Boston Consulting Group has described tandem running as a 'social-learning phenomenon' that works for spreading knowledge within an organisation 'by pairing people who need to learn a skill with more experienced colleagues. As the less experienced employees master the skill, they become change agents for the rest of the team.'[40] This is a 'low effort, high reward' method of knowledge distribution; *if the ants can do it, so can you.*

A good place to start with developing a pairing system is your Organisation Assessment from the Build phase where you collected data on people's 'change readiness' and 'confidence with technology' (see Chapter 6). Someone who feels less at ease with change and systems might really benefit from getting together with someone who does. If you need an argument for those who already feel pretty comfortable with everything and don't see a need to pair up with anyone weaker than themselves, you can always remind them of the 'helper's high' that I mentioned in Chapter 2, or Oppong's 50/50 Rule, according to which you can remember 90% of what you learn if you spend half of your time learning and the other half explaining what you have learned to someone else.[41]

Checklist 2: What to do during go-live

Think of the time of go-live as a high-intensity version of the period before. The earlier tasks remain critically important but pay special attention to these three:

- Make sure that the live support channel is ready and primed to process a high volume of support requests without significant delays.

- Provide your change agents with materials that highlight who they are – think branded t-shirts, cupcakes and banners – as they walk the hallways, so that they can be spotted instantly and called upon to help with urgent matters.

- Have the IT desk on speed dial to call for troubleshooting if larger technical glitches occur as your product or process goes live.

The days of the actual transition should feel like a celebration or festival, a once-in-a-lifetime event that makes people proud to participate and eager for it to succeed. If you've got a tiny bit of money left in your budget, think of ways to make this a particularly pleasant week at your organisation with goodies and giveaways, perhaps a little party after Day One, and definitely a few flower bouquets for those who have worked their butts off for you. And it's never a bad idea to serve free cake, is it?

Checklist 3: What to do after go-live

Once the new product or process has gone live, people have become comfortable, more or less, with their new work routines and some of the craziness has subsided, it is incredibly important for you to ensure that the business change becomes embedded into your organisation's operations in a sustainable, durable and realistic manner, meaning that the new product or process reaches full business-as-usual status. To provide your project's work with the necessary longevity and resilience, you need to be able to transfer both your knowledge and insights, and the ongoing responsibility of the product or process, over to the existing support teams in your organisation (such as the IT desk, the L&D centre or your organisation's equivalent).

To ensure a successful knowledge and responsibility transfer:

- Remind your support teams that the transfer time is approaching.

- Inform them of the long-term strategy for the product or process.

- Prepare support agreements with your vendor for future consultation and maintenance work.

- Prepare a project report to transfer all relevant knowledge.

- Prepare the necessary paperwork to transfer formal ownership.

- Arrange professional training for the new internal owner, budget permitting; otherwise plan a few days for you to walk them through every inch of the system yourself.

- Share all existing content that is to be published on the knowledge platform.

- Advise on how to keep the knowledge platform up to date and engaging over time, making connections with content specialists from Marketing if necessary.

- Keep your change agents well briefed about the handover, so they know their new point of contact in the respective support teams.

And just like that, it's done. You've gone live with your own business change.

This is a big moment for you and you're allowed to pat yourself on the back for giving the power to the people and navigating through the kind of change storm that the world (or at least your organisation) has never seen before.

I am almost loathe to say it because you're probably totally exhausted right now, but while you try to catch your breath and bask in your preliminary success, you need to brace yourself for any unexpected loops or sudden dips that might lie ahead. Needless to say, you have tried to anticipate and prepare for all eventualities, but the world has a funny habit of throwing you a few curveballs even so. Also remember that in a few days' time you will be using the ABC Scorecards to reassess people's performance and understand whether the first round of learning was sufficient or if there's a need to initiate a second, or even a third, coaching cycle.

It would be totally amazing to be done right now, drop the mic and exit the stage, but that is not always how business change processes work, sadly.

CASE STUDY: RIVER CONSTRUCTION

The staff of River Construction needed to learn using a variety of different styles, formats and mediums, so with a small amount of resources allocated from the L&D department budget, I needed to ensure that the materials were as useful as possible for the teams.

I created easy-to-follow PDF guides showing how to use the products, step-by-step.

I provided clear visuals explaining what tools were to be used and when, and these visuals were included in every Microsoft PowerPoint presentation to ensure that the messaging was kept consistent and that information became embedded through repetition.

I also provided online videos that can be sampled here:

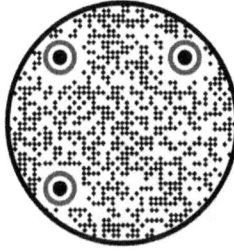

Finally, each week we ran a number of training events, including live sessions, webinars and one-to-one training meetings, all scheduled to a set time each day or week, depending on where we were during the project:

Join our live webinar to learn more about
Microsoft Teams and Yammer

An example of an invitation to a live webinar

Build, Excite, Equip.

Don't forget, all of these training resources were presented on our knowledge platform, available for all to access whenever and wherever:

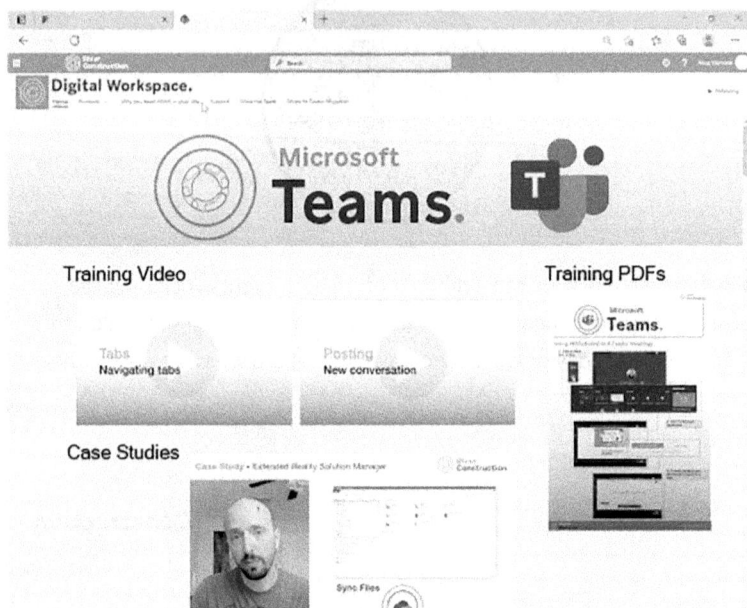

A learning page from River Construction's knowledge platform showing the training information available

21

INVIGORATE
SUSTAINING CHANGE

The final part of the Equip phase, straight after all the training and coaching of the Educate stage, is the period that I like to call Invigorate. This stretch of the change process is dedicated to strengthening confidence, consolidating knowledge, reinforcing routines, cementing the new status quo, fortifying team spirit and celebrating what is a gigantic collective success. After all, you have brought people together for the undertaking of the century.

Maybe that's a little strong... Even if it isn't quite that monumental, at least you have brought about a working life upgrade that makes things at your organisation better, whether that be via more reliable software, a cleaner interface, more efficient communication tools, the introduction of a long-desired functionality that finally brings your organisation into the digital age, or some other technological solution that supports and enhances people's working processes.

Your next step is to go back to the beginning by returning to the good old ABC Scorecards. Remember those? Your project's performance metrics. The ABC Scorecards are the project-specific scores of adoption success that earlier gave every person involved in or affected by the business change a unique score, capturing their progress in Adoption, encouraging them to Be Aware of the project benefits and assessing their Competence. You ran this test for the first time in the Build stage, as an assessment of your project's general standing within the organisation, and now you're going to run it again to see what has changed. The beauty of the ABC Scorecard is that its simple radar-style chart lets you create an overlay of 'then' and 'now' so you can instantly see how the individual parameters have evolved over time.

As anybody with the slightest bit of managerial intuition will deduce, you want people to have improved on their earlier scores, with as many as possible now achieving high scores across all three dimensions. Only when people are adopting the new solution skilfully and with a clear understanding of what's in it for them can the change be sustained beyond the transition phase. Just for the sake of the expectation-management record, I should tell you that, realistically, you probably won't end up with a bunch of perfect isosceles triangles immediately.

A well-acclimatised person's scores after adoption and with a high score in each domain, would look something like this:

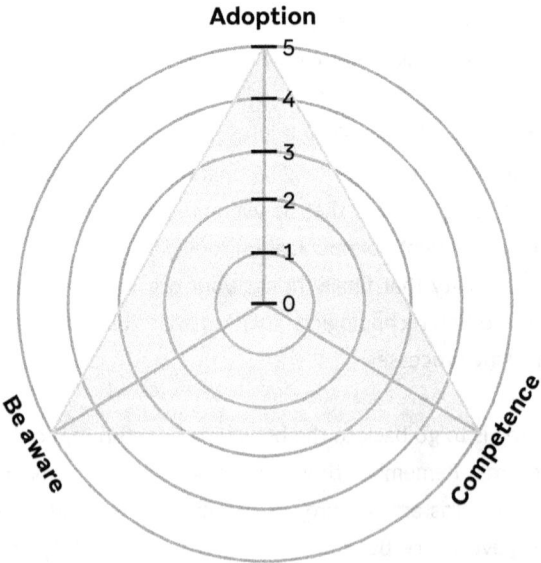

An ABC Scorecard from a well-acclimatised individual, completed after adoption has begun

To find out how A, B and C have improved at your organisation since before adoption began (my, it's been one long journey), you now send out the same questionnaire from the Build phase once again.

The score for this second ABC Scorecard assessment should demonstrate a significant improvement on this individual's first scores; if not, then this is an indication that this individual may need more one-to-one help and support.

Here are the results from the same individual, now with the 'before' and 'after' adoption scores overlaid. This demonstrates a clear increase in the scores for each of the three areas.

Scorecard

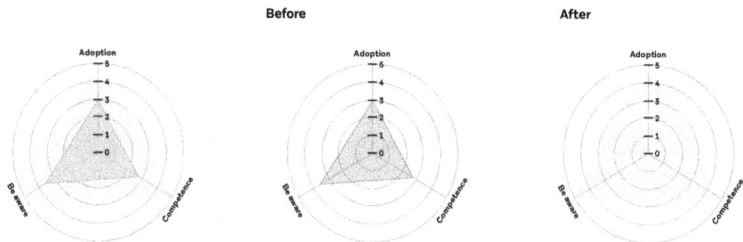

Results (overlaid) of two ABC Scorecards from the same individual, one completed before and one after adoption

An overlaid image like this is an excellent way of reporting success to a project board. You can also create an image showing the average results across the key stakeholders for a more holistic view of the project impact. If you have somehow, achieved a majority of large and balanced triangles that look beautifully uniform across the board, then you and your people magically made this business change happen in just one go and you can move straight to the next section.

If, on the other hand, you get the results back and find yourself looking at some rather wild looking shapes that nowhere near resemble an equilateral triangle, then you're looking at your first data set that will be used to inform the strategy document for the Coach 2.0 Cycle.

The Coach 2.0 Cycle: Once a coach, always a coach

It's quite normal for business change projects not to be totally completed on the first try: it is challenging to ask people to move from one way of working to another overnight, and it's just not how people – or most of us, anyway – tend to function. If you can change your routines at the flip of a switch instead of going through an excruciating couple of months trying to form a new habit, lucky you. The rest of us, however, are only human, and in the face of change we sometimes need a minute to stop, drink a really strong cup of coffee, and then take a second shot at learning.

Here's a simple set of steps to scheme and strategise for your second pass:

1. Visualise individual data sets as 'radar charts' – *if you haven't done so already.*

2. Visualise team/department/division data as aggregated radar charts – *this is the 'bigger picture' stuff.*

3. Move between the individual and aggregated charts to detect whether there are patterns in the data – *you're looking for single occurrences and collective tendencies.*

4. Identify where people's performance is below expectation or the necessary standard – *these should become your next areas of focus.*

5. Go and talk to your connections, your change agents but also people who underwent the standard training and coaching programmes, to find out what's going on and consider where you might have missed something, provided more practical information or simply communicated things differently – *you should take this learning forward.*

6. Meet with your project team and change agents to discuss the Coach 2.0 Cycle, including when to get started, what to focus on, where to change strategy and how to communicate the second round to the rest of the organisation.

7. Gather up all your courage, activate that stamina and go again.

What's really playing in your favour here is that you've already gone through one coaching cycle and probably learned a thing or two about your organisation and your project along the way. You might also have gotten closer to your people and found out about their ('highly individual', let us say) approaches to learning. Now you simply need to recycle what you already know and hone your coaching strategy accordingly. Once the Coach 2.0 Cycle is complete, run the ABC Scorecard test again, and so on. Not exactly a piece of cake, but definitely doable.

Something that I've found absolutely fundamental at this stage, whether or not it inaugurates the project's phasing out, is spicing up the learning materials, so that's what I'll turn to next.

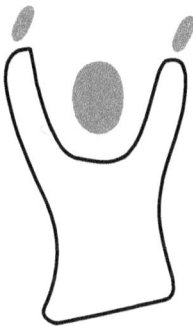

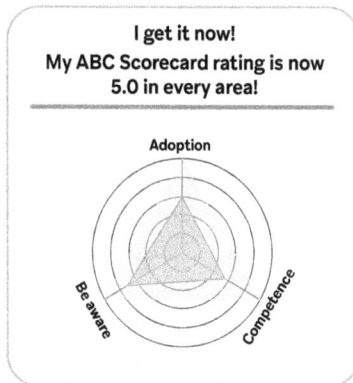

Creating change content

Your business change is continuing to keep people on their toes, either via the expectation of more learning through the Coach 2.0 Cycle, or with the business-as-usual attitude as you begin approaching and concluding the Equip phase. Now is therefore the time when you need to get busy with maintaining enthusiasm and keeping up the good spirit and collective energy. The BEE way of doing that is through the thing that humans find most compelling: stories.

Introducing stories and new content is invaluable, whatever your current position along the change process. When setting out to do a second (or third) round of coaching to get those ABC Scorecards up to speed after some disappointing initial results, creating new content will stop people from feeling as if they're being made to do the same tedious and frustrating tasks all over again. Changing things up is crucial, firstly because something about Coach 1.0 Cycle clearly didn't quite work for them, but also because this must not feel like a punishment with them being made to redo work that was not up to an acceptable standard the first time. You still have to present the same information, of course, but you'll need to be able to repackage it and provide additional inspiration and hacks to make people feel as though this time will be different. Strategic crafting and using careful placement of case studies and success stories with the new product or process is a totally different approach to engaging people in the learning process, and one which may just resonate with those that the Coach 1.0 Cycle passed by.

The opposite is also true. When you and your people have had a pretty good first coaching cycle and adoption success rates are approaching satisfactory, introducing new content in the form of stories is a powerful way of reinforcing the change, creating a sense of collective accomplishment and rewarding those who have sweated blood and tears for you. As bizarre as it may sound, it's also a way of (slowly but surely) beginning the transition into a new status quo, saying goodbye to the work of the last weeks and months, letting go and moving on.

If you've been an attentive reader, and I have no doubt you have, you've probably noticed the subtle shift in my vocabulary from 'learning materials' to 'content'. This movement is quite deliberate and in line with the overall purpose of the Invigorate stage, which has been to bring the business change to life and make some of the 'fluffier' stuff introduced in the Educate stage more tangible. In that sense, think of content creation as the kind of work that lets you fill your everyday life with stories from your neighbourhood, your family and friends, your 'frenemies', your fellow digital currency traders and the computer experts. 'Content' is anything from a news article or an update on social media, to the recipe for a Sunday roast on some legendary chef's food blog. It is any image, recording or piece of writing (or a combination thereof), with or without emojis and hashtags, that you scroll through on websites and numerous apps every single day. Now you're going to jump on the bandwagon and start making your own.

Your task at this stage is to seek out people's stories about your project, capturing what has happened to them over the course of the last weeks and months, sneaking a peek behind the scenes of everyday operations, and gathering it all in a new 'Updates' section on the knowledge platform. This is a journalist-slash-marketing exercise, but also a little like a search engine optimisation (SEO) exercise, because you shouldn't miss the opportunity to draw links between the learning materials and content.

This is an opportunity for you to give change a face and a voice by presenting it through different people's stories, letting them share their experiences from a range of different 'insider' perspectives. A sweet additional benefit of this is that stories tend to stick in our minds and memories better than anything else. You can find lots of scientific explanations of why humans are so attracted to stories and why, to put it simply, they work on us. Storytelling has always been key to our culture, as our early history of societies gathering around bonfires to share experiences and spread knowledge through stories demonstrates. Studies reveal all kinds of benefits related to stories and storytelling in an organisational context, ranging from fostering of collaboration and strengthening a sense of companionship and togetherness, to an increased release of the happiness chemical oxytocin. A quick online search will get you hundreds of thousands of results.[42]

Without meaning any harm, I do consider us and the average project manager-turned-business change manager to be mere laypeople in content creation. Our focus is on timelines, budgets and KPIs, not on pixels, letters and emojis. Don't let that disappoint you – because neither of us are going to be the next Content Creator of the Year, we're allowed to produce stuff that is a little rough around the edges, somewhat ordinary and pretty low budget, as long as it is still in keeping with the strong identity we created for the project.

Despite this 'get out', we do want to present something that will provide genuine support to our project. My secret recipe for creating solid content is, I like to say, SIMPLE:

S	Structured	Nobody can follow an unedited interview, trust me.
I	Inspiring	Include the kind of stuff that makes people go 'Wow!'
M	Meaningful	Your content won't matter if it's irrelevant.
P	Personal	Honesty and humour go a long way.
L	Legible	Keep it intelligible – no gobbledygook or job-specific gibberish.
E	Empathetic	Emotions make all the difference. Tug at those heartstrings.

In other words, there are several considerations to bear in mind when writing your SIMPLE story:

- People need to be able to follow your line of thought, so careful use of subheadings, bold and italics is recommended.

- Your story should motivate and engage people, drawing them in to find out more. Remember to think: what is their inspiration for action?

- The core of your story should be relevant to people's own working lives. This is the time to obtain stories from ordinary people too to ensure a good range of experiences are depicted.

- Ensure that the delivery of your story isn't too sanitised or devoid of its humanity – you're aiming to tell real stories of real people.

- The language of your stories should be accessible to and easily understood by anyone in the organisation. Use the vocabulary that you hear in the hallways and canteen to 'keep it real'.

- Your story should make room for people's feelings during the time of change, even the difficult ones. The Change Curve would be a good place to start to better understand the emotions that may potentially have been involved.

If you're at a loss right now, unable to transition from thinking of yourself as a content consumer to a content creator, do give my SIMPLE method a try. In case of emergency, there's always Kim and the team in Marketing if you get completely stuck. *Time for another lunchtime crash course perhaps?*

The SIMPLE way has proven a successful strategy for me.

If you're struggling for inspiration, remember that content pieces can include almost anything: interviews with people who have been involved in or affected by the change (recorded as audio/video or simply transcribed into the text); blog articles that explore a frequently experienced problem and outline possible solutions; those dreaded, but sometimes necessary, company newsletters with weekly/monthly/seasonal updates; images or interactive polls on your organisation's internal media channels (think of how the notorious social media platforms get people to engage); recycled posts on relevant and pertinent subjects from media outlets or your vendors.

My favourite thing to do is sharing people's top tips. Because everyone explores the new product or process in their own way, people often make individual discoveries or find 'hacks' and shortcuts that don't always appear in the generic overall training. The LinkedIn *2018 Workplace Learning Report* also found that manager involvement matters,[43] so do give your CEO or chief operating officer (COO) a nudge and swing by for a quick interview.

Entering the new normal: The process of business as usual

Here is one more thing for your handover agenda, because this one often slips through the cracks. As your project is getting close to completion and other initiatives are starting to take over as hot topics within the organisation, your new product or process will be joining the family of commonly used solutions that together support business as usual (BAU). Inevitably this means that, before too long, your designated project team is going to move on to other deployments and stop monitoring and analysing every detail concerning the new product or process. This is tricky because BAU is, in fact, the longest and most important phase of the software delivery life cycle. This is obviously because all operations rely on continuous access and use, updates, and uninterrupted technical functionality if they are to survive long term. BAU is therefore the stage of the business change project that is by far the most expensive, simply because licence costs and support expenses add up over time.

To ensure the sustainability of your business change project, it is therefore imperative that the BAU unit at your organisation fully understands the benefits of your product or process and its respective areas of application, and also that it continues to review new functions and features and, when relevant, introduces them to the people. The idea is to thoroughly and continuously exploit the existing solutions to get the most value and economic benefit for the organisation; this is done by simply staying in touch with both the end-users and the program developers.

One little hint: businesses evolve, but so do software products. This is almost a no-brainer.

CASE STUDY: RIVER CONSTRUCTION

At this point in the project, I returned to all the managers that I met at the start, demonstrated the successful uptake within their teams by comparing the ABC scores, and presented them with some of the valued members of staff that had really helped invigorate and support the change. This gave the managers the opportunity once again to outline the success of

Invigorate
the project, with their teams and their peers, and to nominate particular individuals for awards.

Knowing that a bit of friendly rivalry between department heads always kicks off a sense of FOMO ('fear of missing out'), I played this to our advantage by sharing podcasts and interviews with the internal communication teams to spread the word quicker and encourage a bit of healthy competition. I was careful to ensure that I provided emails that were easy to forward and exciting to read: by using HTML, my emails stood out in the inbox, drawing in the reader and powerfully promoted the success of the project.

Microsoft 365 Project Success

GK ○ **Gerald Killam<Gerald.killam@riverconstruction.com>** Today at 13:36
To: ○ **Change Agent Group**

River
Construction.   Microsoft 365 adoption project

Dear all,

Fantastic News, we have successfully closed the Microsoft 365 adoption project. Thank you to all of your enthusiasm and support throughout the project.

> 90% Of employees have said that they understand how the new products have helped them with their work and feel able to use them comfortably.
>
> 85% Feel that collaboration has improved.

Kay Brownfield, Head of HR says:

" I feel I can be much more productive with these products and work more effectively with my team across the globe"

Remember you will always be able to find training resources, help and support on our knowledge platform riverconstruction.sharepoint.com/digitalworkplace

I am sure you will join me in thanking the project team with all their hard work in ensuring the products were rolled out to you in an effective and timely manner.

Kind regards,
Gerald Killam

An email from River Construction communicating the success of the M365 adoption project

I also discovered within River Construction that people enjoy watching their colleagues tell stories, so what better way than to create case studies and newspaper articles specifically to show individuals successes and experiences within the change:

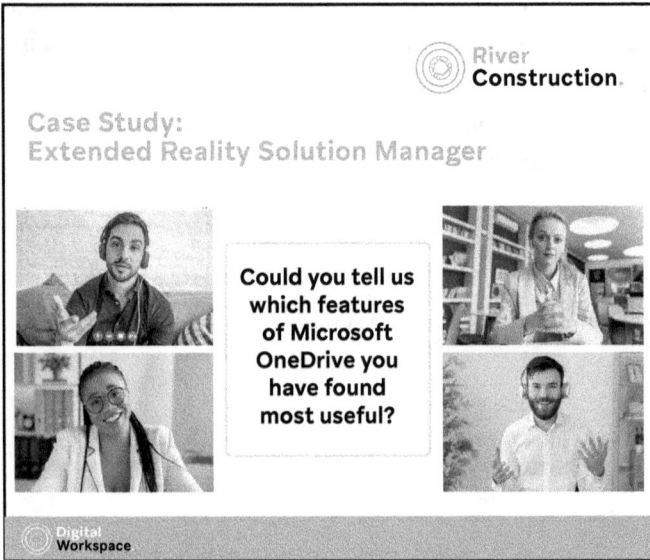

Screenshot from a podcast featuring an interview with a colleague who is positive about the change

Summary

The Invigorate stage is the time to reflect on the success of the project so that you can strengthen confidence, consolidate knowledge and reinforce routines. It is the moment to return to your ABC Scorecards and identify where people need a little more support to truly embed the changes. It's also the time when you can start to celebrate your success, and that of everyone in the organisation who has also successfully navigated the journey of change with you.

EQUIP PHASE SUMMARY

Develop

○ Develop your knowledge platform:

— Who is learning?

— What will they be learning?

— What do they need to learn?

— How will they learn?

— How will they maintain what they have learned?

○ Develop the skills of your change agents:

— Who is learning?

— What will they be learning?

— What do they need to learn?

— How will they learn?

— How will they maintain what they have learned?

Educate

○ The Coach 1.0 Cycle

○ Checklist 1: What to do before go-live

○ Checklist 2: What to do during go-live

○ Checklist 3: What to do after go-live

Invigorate

○ Adoption Success Rating

○ The Coach 2.0 Cycle

○ Create change content

○ BAU Process

PART V
REFLECTION

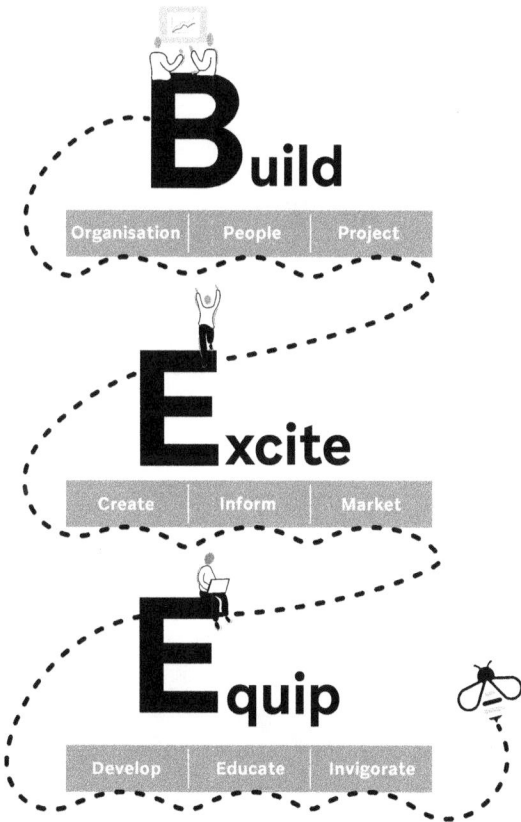

Build

| Organisation | People | Project |

Excite

| Create | Inform | Market |

Equip

| Develop | Educate | Invigorate |

22

MOVING ON
THE NEXT PHASE

You have now officially gone through an entire BEE cycle with your business change project and done the unimaginable at your organisation: over the last few weeks or months (although it may feel like a whole lifetime right now), you have successfully united and carried the diverse-as-heck crowd to pull off a spectacular habit-forming and future-preparing stunt. You have set your organisation on the right course going forward and ensured everyone is safely on board; in our change projects, we leave nobody on shore.

This final stage, equipping people to operate under a whole new status quo, is some of the most challenging stuff I've seen project managers co-ordinate and conquer. It takes a well-organised person to map out a business change project, but it takes a kind-hearted, committed, entirely convincing, endlessly empathetic, incredibly resourceful and remarkably resilient person to successfully carry through a business change project that affects the working lives of so many. It probably wasn't always easy, but you've done it: you've arrived. You must have heard your fair share of expletives along the way. Heaven knows, I have, but that's part of the process.

Recycle everything you've got

However much you struggled with your crowd along the way, and whatever trouble kept you tossing and turning at night, you have made it this far, but now what? So much time went into building an understanding of the organisation and the people behind it, so much effort went into exciting people for the project through branding, campaigning and connecting it across the organisation, and now, all of the sudden, you have already gone through one (or two, or more) coaching cycles and the new product or process is up and running. Don't think now is the moment to plant that flag and admire the view; activity is all around you. You'll probably find that it feels a bit like having breathlessly rushed up Mount Everest in only three days, only then to go whirling down like a deflating balloon in less than ten seconds?

Here's something to remember and internalise at this point: you may have reached the summit, but you don't need to hang up your climbing boots; *after all, it's only now that they're starting to fit comfortably, right?* Now is your opportunity to recycle and work through any of the previous phases and stages to your heart's content, should there still be room for improvement. We all know that recycling is what we do these days and the sustainable choice to make. 'Upcycle', 'renovate', 'repurpose' and 'transform' your skills and knowledge, to make something new and improved from what was there before. Just because you've gone through the BEE once (and the coaching cycle at least that), this doesn't mean that you must now leave things as they are.

Using the latest ABC scores as your strategic compass, now is the moment to consider if an improvement of, or even a new incarnation for, the change project remains. Consider whether some of your existing project resources can be fed into the system again; you have done most of the hard work already. For example, if your adoption progress is not exactly mind-blowing, let people know how others are reinventing their workflows using the new solution (you've already got those interviews); if the awareness of the benefits is underwhelming, run a marketing campaign with a specific focus on the advantages that it will bring (the brand identity is sitting in some folder just waiting to be used); and if the level of Competence could be better, reintegrate active learning into people's schedules and send out daily tutorials that target key features for BAU operations (you should have a heap of learning materials to choose from). Afterwards – *you guessed it* – why not run the scorecards again? Practice (ie repetition) makes perfect, as everybody knows.

As an aside, it would probably be a good move to give the BAU unit access to all the resources, assets and learning that you have accumulated over the course of the project – questions, questionnaires, evaluations, assessments, results, brand assets etc; this is in addition to

> Use, reuse and use again what you have already. And feel inspired to use what you have beyond the project end date.

the formal documents and signatures that come with the official handover. Thinking ahead to what they might need in the future is the final million-dollar move that you can make for your project.

Looking forward

You may find it a little difficult to let go of all of your incredible work; this project has generated impressive results and you should be rightly proud of your achievements. Handing it over and leaving it to others can feel as gut-wrenching and heart-pounding as leaving your child for their first day at school, even though you know logically that all will go will. Whether to the best school in the area or the critical team that assures smooth operations at your organisation every day, you are entrusting your baby to somebody else, and that is a difficult moment for anyone.

Remember here that what you are experiencing is a kind of loss: this is *the end of something big* and that absence will be felt in many ways. This is the loss of the extremely strong sense of purpose that comes with business change management; the loss of a unique team spirit generated just from these people working on this project and never to be felt again; it is the loss of the identity as the person undertaking a massive change that will change the lives of people across the organisation for the better, and the resulting pride that came from being, and being recognised as, that person.

This is not a 'what goes around, comes around' kind of comment, even if it may sound like it; rather it is a reminder that you, too, are human. While you have become a strong and sensible professional, you are also a person, with all the vulnerabilities and frailties, whose identity and sense of self-worth is partly fed by the appreciation of others and an inherent need to belong. You may be a leader, but you also want to form part of enduring social relationships, and the end of the project can seem like a moment when all of that is at risk.

Let me assure you that this natural process of concluding and rounding out is the way things go in business change management: you cook up what sounds like an exceptionally good idea; get permission from above to throw a spanner in the works; then pull together an amazingly talented project team that grows into a second family. Together you march right through hell trying to make the change happen. You realise along the way that your 'exceptionally good idea' is making everything difficult for people, but carry on anyway and campaign until every last person (in what seems like the whole universe) has heard about your project. Next you program a comprehensive, intuitive, creative and innovative online academy and somehow get people to work through it, becoming a half-journalist in the process. Now you need to let someone else take legal authority over your 'baby' and move on with your life. But not until you've had a nice long well-deserved rest.

Or perhaps not, as you may find yourself running straight towards the next mountain and uphill battle that you can find, because you have become quite fond (not to say 'addicted') of tackling the impossibilities that can grow into opportunities, the challenges that unfold into chances, and the uncertainties that lay out the course towards the future. That is, truthfully, the circle of life of a business change manager, and now, that includes you. Welcome to the Club.

Summary: A note from the trenches

Having addressed the feelings of nostalgia and departure that are inherent to the completion and handover of a project, I'd like to take a second to make you aware of something else that you have gained on this journey from being a project manager to becoming a business change manager. You may have left behind your highly analytical approach and go-go-go attitude, but you have dived headlong into the world of empathy and empowerment. With a complete shift of your priorities, away from the limited focus of time and money and towards a broad people-centred learning orientation, you have made business in this ridiculously fast-paced world a little bit more human.

This is an accomplishment of which you should be extremely proud. We all need more humanity in the organisations we're part of and work for, and at Simplify Change, I truly believe that integrating the technical aspects of project management with the people stuff of business change management is an invaluable step in that direction. Together with the project managers of this world, I want to start building a future where people at organisations feel able, enabled and valued. I want a future where people can make a difference for their colleagues, their colleagues who became friends, and all those who together build the strength and integrity of your teams, the richness and creativity of your departments and the incredible power within your organisation.

> I want a future where people matter. BEE is on a mission to get us there.

NOTES

1   Prosci, *The Importance of Integrating Individual and Organizational Change* (Prosci, 2022), www.prosci.com/resources/articles, accessed July 2022

2   C Huxham, 'Pursuing collaborative advantage', *Journal of the Operational Research Society*, 44/6 (1993), 599–611, https://doi.org/10.1057/jors.1993.101

3   J Liburd, *Towards the Collaborative University: Lessons from tourism education and research* (professorial dissertation) (University of Southern Denmark, 2013), www.researchgate.net/publication/262536122_Towards_the_Collaborative_ University_Lessons_from_Tourism_Education_and_Research_Proefssorial_ Dissertation_Odense_Print_Sign, accessed June 2022

4   Deloitte, *The Collaborative Economy* (Deloitte, 2014), www2.deloitte.com/ content/dam/Deloitte/au/Documents/Economics/deloitte-au-economics-collaborative-economy-google-170614.pdf, accessed July 2022

5   HermanMiller, *What It Takes to Collaborate* (Herman Miller, 2012), www. hermanmiller.com/content/dam/hermanmiller/documents/research_summaries/ wp_What_It_Takes_to_Collaborate.pdf, accessed June 2022

6   HermanMiller, *What It Takes to Collaborate*, 3

7   L Dossey, 'The helper's high', *EXPLORE: The Journal of Science and Healing*, 14/6 (October 2018), 393–399, www.researchgate.net/publication/328460127_The_ Helper's_High, accessed June 2022

8   F Frei, 'How to build (and rebuild) trust', *TED: Ideas worth spreading* (2018), www.ted.com/talks/frances_frei_how_to_build_and_rebuild_trust?referrer=playlist-the_most_transformative_ted_talks, accessed June 2022

9   PwC, 'Redefining business success in a changing world', *19th Annual Global CEO Survey*, PwC (January 2016), 7, www.pwc.com/gx/en/ceo-survey/2016/ landing-page/pwc-19th-annual-global-ceo-survey.pdf, accessed June 2022

10   H Koontz and C O'Donnell, *Principles of Management: An analysis of managerial functions* (McGraw-Hill, 1960)

11   R Morris and G Ward (Eds), *The Cognitive Psychology of Planning* (Psychology Press, 2005)

12   Project Management Institute, 'Success rates rise: Transforming the high cost of low performance', *PMI's Pulse of the Profession*, (2017), 9, www.pmi.org/-/media/

pmi/documents/public/pdf/learning/thought-leadership/pulse/pulse-of-the-profession-2017.pdf, accessed June 2022

13   SL Friedman and EK Scholnick, 'Preface', In SL Friedman and EK Scholnick (Eds), *The Developmental Psychology of Planning: Why, how, and when do we plan?* (Psychology Press, 2014), xi

14   J-B A Karr, 1862. Cited by HL Sirkin, P Keenan and A Jackson, 'The hard side of change management', *Harvard Business Review* (October 2005), https://hbr.org/2005/10/the-hard-side-of-change-management, accessed June 2022

15   V Lipman, 'The 9 most dangerous words in business', *Forbes* (20 May 2014), www.forbes.com/sites/victorlipman/2014/05/20/the-9-most-dangerous-words-in-business/?sh=2c504ab5975a, accessed June 2022

16   Cambridge Dictionary, 'Neuroscience' (no date), https://dictionary.cambridge.org/dictionary/english/neuroscience, accessed July 2022

17   Merriam Webster Dictionary, 'Neuroscience' (no date), www.merriam-webster.com/dictionary/neuroscience, accessed June 2022

18   D Rock, 'Managing with the brain in mind', *strategy+business*, 56 (Autumn 2009), www.psychologytoday.com/sites/default/files/attachments/31881/managingwbraininmind.pdf, accessed June 2022

19   Rock, 'Managing with the brain in mind', 3

20   M Valcour and J McNulty, 'To make a change at work, tell yourself a different story', *Harvard Business Review* (24 August 2018), https://hbr.org/2018/08/to-make-a-change-at-work-tell-yourself-a-different-story, accessed June 2022

21   Rock, 'Managing with the brain in mind', 6

22   D Rice, 'Generations in the workplace: Statistics show the impact of pandemic by age', *HR Exchange Network* (28 January 2021), www.hrexchangenetwork.com/employee-engagement/articles/generations-in-the-workplace, accessed June 2022

23   Prosci, *7 Compelling Reasons for Deploying Change Management* (Prosci), www.prosci.com/resources/articles, accessed July 2022

24   Chainga (@chaingaz), 'Only 7% of our communication is verbal...' (6 July 2021) https://twitter.com/Chaingaz/status/1412359659336437763, accessed June 2022

25   The Kübler-Ross Change Curve®, EKR Foundation (no date), www.ekrfoundation.org/5-stages-of-grief/change-curve, accessed June 2022

26   E Kübler-Ross, *On Death and Dying* (Routledge, 1969)

27 CC Rosen et al, 'Boxed in by your inbox: Implications of daily e-mail demands for managers' leadership behaviors', *Journal of Applied Psychology*, 104/1 (2019), 19–33, https://doi.org/10.1037/apl0000343

28 C Melore, 'Office outrage: Sending emails "most frustrating task" of the workday', *Study Finds* (4 May 2022), www.studyfinds.org/office-emails-frustrating-tasks-new-job, accessed June 2022

29 *Pacific Standard* staff, 'There's a name for that: The Baader-Meinhof Phenomenon', *Pacific Standard* (14 June 2017), https://psmag.com/social-justice/theres-a-name-for-that-the-baader-meinhof-phenomenon-59670, accessed June 2022

30 S Parrish, 'Social Proof: Why we look to others for what we should think and do', *Farnham Street* blog (no date), https://fs.blog/mental-model-social-proof, accessed June 2022

31 A Dvornechuck, 'Brand? branding? or brand identity?', *Medium* (6 February 2017), https://medium.com/@ebaqdesign/the-differences-betlen-brand-branding-and-brand-identity-726f0510c89c, accessed June 2022

32 Cited by W Arruda, 'The most damaging myth about branding', *Forbes* (6 September 2016), https://www.forbes.com/sites/williamarruda/2016/09/06/the-most-damaging-myth-about-branding/?sh=6c0e52b15c4f, accessed June 2022

33 Dvornechuck, 'Brand? branding? or brand identity?'

34 S Maybin, 'Busting the attention span myth', *BBC News* (10 March 2017), www.bbc.com/news/health-38896790, accessed June 2022

35 Frei, 'How to build (and rebuild) trust'

36 J Baier et al, *Why You Need a New Approach to Learning* (Boston Consulting Group, 3 June 2020), www.bcg.com/publications/2020/why-you-need-new-approach-learning, accessed 2022

37 LinkedIn, *2018 Workplace Learning Report: The rise and responsibility of talent development in the new labor market*, LinkedIn Learning (27 February 2018), https://learning.linkedin.com/resources/workplace-learning-report-2018, accessed June 2022

38 D Krasinski, 'How to tell the difference between coaching and training', *Maestro* (28 December 2018), https://maestrolearning.com/blogs/how-to-tell-the-difference-between-coaching-and-training, accessed June 2022

39 D Krasinski, 'How to tell the difference between coaching and training'

40   Baier et al, *Why You Need a New Approach to Learning*

41   T Oppong, 'The 50/50 Rule (How to retain and remember 90% of everything you learn)', *Pocket* (no date; originally published 5 March 2019), https://getpocket.com/explore/item/the-50-50-rule-how-to-retain-and-remember-90-of-everything-you-learn, accessed June 2022

42   For example, S Denning, 'Effective storytelling: Strategic business narrative techniques', *Strategy & Leadership*, 34/1 (2006), 42–48, https://doi.org/10.1108/10878570610637885; RT Barker and K Gower, 'Strategic application of storytelling in organizations: Toward effective communication in a diverse world', *The Journal of Business Communication*, 47/3 (25 June 2010), 295–312, https://doi.org/10.1177%2F0021943610369782

43   LinkedIn, *2018 Workplace Learning Report*

FURTHER RESOURCES

Behavioral Economics, *Social Proof* (no date), www.behavioraleconomics.com/resources/mini-encyclopedia-of-be/social-proof/, accessed July 2022

Lipman, V, 'Why does organizational change usually fail? New study provides simple answer', *Forbes* (2016), www.forbes.com/sites/victorlipman/2016/02/08/why-does-organizational-change-usually-fail-new-study-provides-simple-answer/, accessed July 2022

MindTools, *Emotional Intelligence. Developing Strong 'People Skills'* (MindTools, no date), www.mindtools.com/pages/article/newCDV_59.htm, accessed 2022

Rich, A, 'What is the Baader-Meinhof Phenomenon?' *The Lighthouse* (Macquarie University, 2020), https://lighthouse.mq.edu.au/article/july-2020/What-is-the-Baader-Meinhof-Phenomenon, accessed July 2022

Sirkin, HL, Keenan P and Jackson A, 'The hard side of change management', *Harvard Business Review* (October 2005), https://hbr.org/2005/10/the-hard-side-of-change-management, accessed July 2022

Thagard, P, 'What is trust? Trust is an emotional brain state, not just an expectation of behavior', *Psychology Today* (9 October 2018), www.psychologytoday.com/us/blog/hot-thought/201810/what-is-trust, accessed July 2022

University of Leicester, 'Inverted pyramid' (no date), www2.le.ac.uk/offices/external/news/publicising/how-to-write-a-press-release/inverted-pyramid, accessed August 2022

van der Linden, S, 'The helper's high: Why it feels so good to give', *Ode Magazine*, 8/6 (2011), 26–27, https://scholar.princeton.edu/slinden/publications/helpers-high-why-it-feels-so-good-give, accessed August 2022

ACKNOWLEDGEMENTS

To my business partner and best friend, Zayn Blore. Thank you for believing in me and encouraging me to create this book, and never giving up on me or the company. Your support, dedication and loyalty to both our company and friendship is truly a lifeline.

To Anna Yeomans, for all of your help putting this book together. Your counsel, assistance and analytical mind has been vital in the completion of this book. You have been inspiring to watch over the past three years. Thank you for teaching me so much. It appears the Padawan has now become the master.

To the rest of the Simplify Change team: Birthe for your incredible insight into book writing, Carlo and Travisha for your visual designs, and Jen and Jam for your marketing and organisational skills. It's been a true team effort. As with most things in my life, I wouldn't be able to do it without great teamwork.

It's been a long journey writing this book, and I have a newfound respect for every author who has ever written a book. It is a marathon, for sure. To ALL my friends, colleagues and loved ones who have supported me with this book. Thank you.

THE AUTHOR

Nicola Graham began her career in sales before transitioning into project management. She has since worked with numerous national and international businesses, FTSE 100 companies, The Big Four consultancies and British government organisations, including the NHS.

In 2019, Nicola founded Simplify Change with Zayn Blore, to support companies such as Deloitte, BSI, Subsea7 and Lloyds Bank manage their change processes, all the while doing what she describes as 'the hardest, most rewarding job in the world' – parenting.

When time permits, you'll find Nicola clocking up huge miles on her road bike, raising money for charities (check out www.sportynicnic.com), or diving deep into oceans and helping to conserve them.

Simply Change (www.simplifychange.co.uk) is a growing company with three main focus areas:

BEE: Adopt focuses on BEE Methodology. The BEE Insights tool is the company's key assessment product which takes the hard work out of analytics to save time and generate data-specific information for change projects. It draws on many years of experience in what to ask and when to ask it.

Build, Excite, Equip.

BEE: Interact is a gaming area. The super-cool leading-edge part of the business is where adoption games are created for flagship products and tailored to client needs. It provides novel, quick and useful ways to help people learn, as well as the analytics needed to support adoption.

BEE: Consult is a consultancy service offering change management support, system leadership and project management skills.

Nicola provides BEE training and consultancy. Get in touch to find out more at info@simplifychange.co.uk

🌐 www.simplifychange.co.uk

in www.linkedin.com/in/nicola-graham-uk

www.ingramcontent.com/pod-product-compliance
Lightning Source LLC
Chambersburg PA
CBHW071542200326
41519CB00021BB/6575